Chuck - Merry Christmas '94

Love, Di

People weekly

CELEBRATES PEOPLE

MEL BROOKS, 1975

STEVE SCHAPIRO

GEORGIA O'KEEFFE, 1975

DAN BUDNIK / WOODFIN CAMP

SPIDER JEWELRY, 1982

CO RENTMEESTER

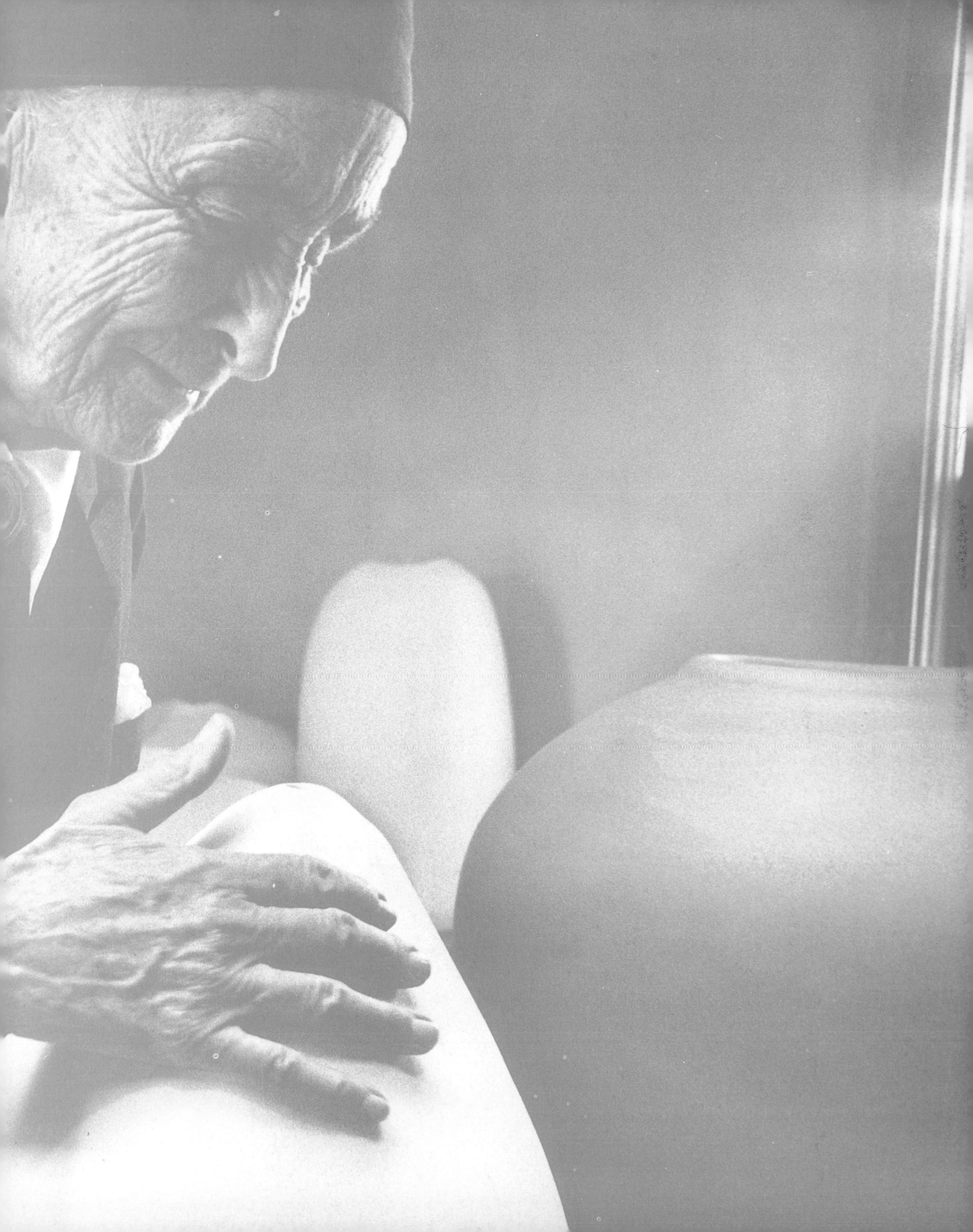

PRESIDENTS GEORGE BUSH, RONALD REAGAN, JIMMY CARTER, GERALD FORD & RICHARD NIXON, 1991

DAVID HUME KENNERLY

VIRGINIA BLYTH CLINTON KELLEY (WITH PORTRAIT OF BILL), 1992

HARRY BENSON

DUDLEY MOORE, 1983

MARK SENNET

MARTHA MITCHELL, 1974

ALFRED EISENSTAEDT

CELEBRATES PEOPLE

THE BEST OF 20 UNFORGETTABLE YEARS

EDITED BY
RICHARD B. STOLLEY

WRITTEN BY TONY CHIU   DESIGNED BY SUSAN MARSH

Published by
People weekly® Books

Distributed by
Little, Brown and Company
Boston • New York • Toronto • London

A Division of Time Inc. Home Entertainment
1271 Avenue of the Americas
New York, NY 10020

First Edition
ISBN 0-316-81815-1
Manufactured in the United States of America

PEOPLE CELEBRATES PEOPLE
Editor: Richard B. Stolley
Writer: Tony Chiu
Designer: Susan Marsh
Picture Editors: Celia Waters, Katherine Bourbeau
Research: Ann Guerin
Copy Editor: Ricki Tarlow
Page Makeup: Matt Mayerchak

Special thanks to: Sarah Brennan, Richard J. Durrell, Daniel F. Farley, Fredrica Friedman, Otto Fuerbringer, Anita Hussey, Ann Jackson, Landon Y. Jones Jr., Paul Livornese, Mary Carroll Marden, Dick Martell, Jim Oberman, Sally Proudfit, Matthew Semble, Candace Stuart, Robert F. Warren Jr. and Delia Chiu; also to Arcata Graphics, Horowitz/Rae, Lanman Progressive, Time Inc. Picture Collection and Time/Life Photo Lab.

PEOPLE CONSUMER MARKETING
Director: Jeremy Koch
Manager: Amy Keonane

NEW BUSINESS DEVELPOMENT
Director: David Gitow
Assistant Director: Mary Warner McGrade
Production Director: John Calvano
Manufacturing Director: David Rivchin

TIME INC. MAGAZINES
Editor-in-Chief: Jason McManus
Editorial Director: Henry Muller

TIME INC.
Chairman, CEO: Reginald K. Brack Jr.
President: Don Logan

Library of Congress Catalog Card Number: 93-80-888
10 9 8 7 6 5 4 3 2 1
Published simultaneously in Canada

IVANA TRUMP & RICCARDO MAZZUCCHELLI, 1992

HARRY BENSON

CONTENTS

GRACE JONES & JEAN PAUL GOUDE, 1979

CO RENTMEESTER

A LETTER FROM THE EDITOR

On *Beverly Hills, 90210,* **SHANNEN DOHERTY** was the bitch goddess Brenda*;* offscreen, she was likewise a rebel without a pause. In 1993 (*above),* after a night club brawl, paycheck garnishments and a sudden marriage to Ashley Hamilton, 19, fed-up producers were mulling over giving their star, 22, a ticket to ride.
LANCE STAEDLER / SYGMA

Daddy Warbucks and Mr. Clean were drawn that way; **TELLY SAVALAS**'s pate was razored smooth. It was part of the raffish persona of a former State Department and ABC News exec who took up acting at age 37. Overcoming his thuggish typecasting (he was the scuzziest of *The Dirty Dozen),* by 1974 (*left)* Savalas, 52, had TV's No. 1 show, *Kojak,* and an Emmy.
MICHAEL MAUNEY

This book began with an idea and a mountain of photographs. The idea was to compile a history of popular culture as reported by PEOPLE magazine since 1974 to mark the publication's 20th birthday. The photographs would be the vehicle for telling the story. They wound up showing us the way, as pictures so often do if editors will only listen with their eyes. My colleagues and I spread the pictures, thousands of them, around a big conference room, on the table, the chairs, the floor. We walked around and through them, debating what approach to take to this mass of material, peering at the images — and listening to them. Then it became clear. SImply do the book the way we had lived the years, day by day, year by year, beginning to end.

As you will see, our definition of pop culture is broad and generous, as the magazine's has always been (some of the credit or blame for this is mine, as PEOPLE's founding editor). As we see it, pop culture is made up of people and performances and events that touch our hearts as well as our heads. An arms-reduction treaty is news but not culture. A baby trapped in a well has both news and a cultural impact. Or so we believe, and the magazine and this book reflect that conviction.

Putting the book together was of course like reliving the past 20 years — a fascinating but not altogether blessed experience. The middle and late '70s seem curiously remote, almost tranquil after the national outrage over Vietnam and racial inequality began to subside. But the dark moments are seen here: the drug wildfire that spread across the land, the disillusionment with authority after Watergate, the decade ending with our special domestic brand of violence, the handgun murder of John Lennon on a Manhattan sidewalk.

The '80s proved that greed, to paraphrase a famous observation, is as American as apple pie. Some people made a lot of money; a lot of people didn't. But with the money came a conspicuous consumption of pop culture. Government funding may have dried up to a degree; private spending and funding were lavish. Many of the arts flourished, and before the decade was over a few of pop culture's most generous patrons went to jail for getting rich by breaking the law.

And now the '90s are here, sober, self-searching, subdued, the hangover decade, not least for the appalling toll of AIDS among pop culture's most creative talents. And yet, in spite of all the signals for change being hoisted in Washington, the '90s feel almost like throwaway time, an impatient countdown to the 21st century and all the marvels we have been promised.

If I make the past 20 years sound somber and barely survivable, I do not mean to. In many ways and on many days, they were quite wonderful. The irrepressibly inventive American spirit shone through. We played rock louder and better, and adopted or coopted foreign rivals. We walked pet rocks and wore

At age 5, **LISA MARIE PRESLEY** was living with Mom **PRISCILLA** in Los Angeles (*right*) but logging visitation time with Dad in Memphis; she was 9 when Elvis died. By 1993, Lisa Marie (*left*) had become the married mother of two, a Scientologist and, at 25, sole heir to her father's $100 million estate. She had also quietly cut four demo tapes that were, by some accounts, more than respectable. Perhaps the King will indeed live again.

CURT GUNTHER / PETER BORSARI (RIGHT); DICK ZIMMERMAN

mood rings. We encouraged country music to cross over. We created movies and television that the whole world watched (not without complaints). We produced world tennis champions and welcomed defecting ballet stars. We took a French-speaking pig to heart. We delighted in Caroline Kennedy's happy marriage, and the end of Warren Beatty's bachelor days too. We learned to savor the fiery delights of sinus-clearing Cajun cooking. We rejoiced in the fact that Bart Simpson wasn't our kid. We forgave Madonna.

In pop culture's house are many mansions. To help you tour them, here is our guide. Be prepared for the shock of the old ("I forgot Jonestown happened *that* year!") and the joy of the new ("Wasn't Bill Gates *adorable* back then?"). Be prepared for belly laughs and moist eyes. Be prepared for a fresh appreciation of the artistic and emotional turbulence of the past 20 years as covered by PEOPLE — coverage that has been, I hope you will agree, perceptive, skeptical, good-natured and kind. Be prepared for the most enjoyable history lesson of your life.

Richard B. Stolley

Endgame in a 26-month melodrama: The day before resigning the presidency, **RICHARD M. NIXON** addressed his White House staff; flanking him were wife **PAT,** daughter **TRICIA NIXON COX** and son-in-law **EDWARD COX.** Nixon was about to be impeached for his role in covering up a politically motivated 1972 burglary at Washington's Watergate complex.

HARRY BENSON

1974

A funny thing happened to 13-term Congressman **JERRY FORD,** 61, on the way to retirement: the White House. Assuming the presidency vacated by Nixon on August 9, Ford's informality (like his impromptu dip with pooch Liberty) was tonic to a Watergate-weary nation. That openness extended to the entire family; in an act of candor remarkable for the time, wife Betty revealed her breast cancer and underwent a mastectomy (leaving high school senior **SUSAN,** 17, to pinch-hit as First Hostess). Lampoonists loved the new Chief Executive's penchant for tripping on steps and nailing spectators with errant golf shots, and no one enjoyed the spoofs more than Ford. Yet the misstep that couldn't be laughed off—one that hovered like Banquo's ghost over the rest of his unexpected presidency—was the unconditional pardon Ford granted his predecessor in the Oval Office.

FRED WARD / BLACK STAR

America confronts — and handsomely survives — a constitutional crisis without parallel in the first 182 years of the republic. Between October 10, 1973, and December 19, 1974, although there is neither a general election nor death in high office, the nation's leadership is shared by three Vice Presidents (two of them appointed) and two Presidents (one of them unelected). Less than a year after Richard Nixon and Spiro Agnew are returned to the White House with the second greatest plurality in U.S. history, Agnew refuses to contest charges of having solicited bribes during his first term as Vice President and resigns. The Senate confirms as his successor Representative Gerald Ford of Michigan, who 10 month later, with Nixon irreparably damaged by Watergate, moves into 1600 Pennsylvania Avenue. Ford chooses as his Vice President former New York governor Nelson Rockefeller.

At this moment, the Dow-Jones stands at 797.6; home mortgages are available at 9.2 percent; the sticker on a new two-door Chevy reads $2,527 (foreign-made cars claim but 16 percent of the market); milk averages 44¢ a quart and bread 59¢ a loaf; a first-class stamp costs 10¢. Yet the new Administration's immediate priority is whipping inflation, now. The chief culprit behind the rising cost of living is surging oil prices. Before the late-1973 Yom Kippur War, in which four Arab nations attacked Israel, Americans were paying 37¢ a gallon for gas; now, with the OPEC cartel embargoing shipments of crude, motorists must queue up to fill their tanks at the doomsday price of 53¢ a gallon.

Two of the year's blockbuster movies are also apocalyptic: *Earthquake* and *The Towering Inferno,* known collectively in Hollywood as "Shake and Bake." The earth moves for CBS too. A new sitcom spun off from *The Mary Tyler Moore Show* draws 50 million viewers for Episode 8, in which *Rhoda* (Valerie Harper) marries Joe (David Groh). Baseball also has a breakthrough year. Frank Robinson, 39, becomes the first black major-league manager (but of the hapless Cleveland Indians; gee, thanks). And on April 8, at Atlanta-Fulton County Stadium, Braves slugger Henry Aaron, 40, hammers a hanging Al Downing curveball into the left-field bleachers for home run No. 715, one more than Babe Ruth.

Passages: Jack Benny, 80. Scientist and PBS host Jacob Bronowski, 66. Duke Ellington, 75. Longtime NBC news anchor Chet Huntley, 62. Charles Lindbergh, 73 (47 years after his epochal trans-Atlantic solo and 42 years after the kidnap-murder of his son). German industrialist Oskar Schindler, 66 (who during World War II saved some 1,300 Jews from Hitler's death camps, a feat remembered in Steven Spielberg's powerful 1993 movie). Poet Anne Sexton, 45. Nuclear industry whistle-blower Karen Silkwood, 28. TV master of ceremonies Ed Sullivan, 73.

Among the 183 graduates of Yale Law School: Clarence Thomas, 25. Making his motion-picture debut in the surf's-up epic *Sizzle Beach*: Kevin Costner, 19. In Oceanside, New York, furniture upholsterer Elliot Fisher and his wife, Roseann, welcome their first child, whom they name Amy. And in Arkansas, veteran Representative John Hammerschmidt, 52, staves off the challenge of a 28-year-old first-time office seeker; consoling loser Bill Clinton is a staff lawyer on the House Watergate committee whom he has been courting, Hillary Rodham.

At 10, TATUM O'NEAL became Oscar's youngest winner by copping Best Supporting Actress for *Paper Moon;* she was the Depression-era waif who falls in with a con man, played by real-life dad Ryan O'Neal. (In a short-lived 1974 TV spinoff of the movie, Tatum's role was filled by Jodie Foster.)

PAUL SLAUGHTER

At 32 a veteran of the civil rights movement, the Rev. **JESSE JACKSON** was now focusing on Operation PUSH. He had founded the Chicago-based economic bootstrap organization upon his split from the Southern Christian Leadership Conference following the 1968 slaying of Martin Luther King Jr.

MICHAEL MAUNEY

When Soviet writer **ALEXANDER SOLZHENITSYN** won the 1970 Nobel Prize for such antitotalitarian novels as *The Cancer Ward* and *First Circle,* it cost him his citizenship. In 1974, Moscow sent Solzhenitsyn, then 55, into exile; after two years in Switzerland, he settled in Vermont and finished his three-volume epic, *The Gulag Archipelago.*

JEAN-CLAUDE FRANCOLON / GAMMA-LIAISON

Even as **CATHERINE** and **RANDOLPH HEARST** strove to meet the demands of the terrorists who had kidnapped their daughter **PATTY,** the newspaper heiress, 19, posed for a snapshot (*inset*) militantly garbed as "Citizen Tania" of the Symbionese Liberation Army. Patty remained underground for 19 months before turning herself in. Convicted of armed robbery, she served 22 months in jail.

ASSOCIATED PRESS

MIA FARROW won the most coveted role, as Daisy, in the year's most hyped movie. Alas, *The Great Gatsby,* starring Robert Redford, bombed —but not before the actress, 29 and still wed to second husband André Previn, became the first cover subject of PEOPLE.

STEVE SCHAPIRO

Stripped of his heavyweight boxing crown in 1969 for refusing service in Vietnam, **MUHAMMAD ALI** reclaimed it at age 32 with an eighth-round knockout of 26-year-old George Foreman in Zaire. Ali retired in 1981 with a career record of 56 wins and five losses.

CO RENTMEESTER

At 5' 8½", **ELTON JOHN** required mega-platform shoes to play the "Pinball Wizard" in the big-screen version of The Who's rock opera, *Tommy.* The British star, 27, needed no such lift in his recording career; *Caribou,* John's newly released 10th album, had just gone platinum.

TERRY O'NEILL

Sharing the first dance reserved by Wimbledon for its new singles champs were two-fisted baseline tactician **CHRIS EVERT,** 19, and her fiancé, quick-tempered lefty **JIMMY CONNORS,** 22. But the romance that launched a thousand tennis puns ended with a double-fault; both married others, reuniting only for a painkiller ad.

PRESS ASSOCIATION

The fad of **STREAKING** discombobulated bobbies at a rugby match in Twickenham, England (*right*); the NBC crew televising the 1974 Oscars (at which a naked gent interrupted co-host David Niven in mid-sentence); and campus cops coast to coast. Have pity, too, on all the photo editors who had to search for an image fit to print.

GLOBE

In 1963 he was the bare-legged tyke in a short Chesterfield coat who rebroke a nation's heart by bravely saluting the casket of his assassinated father. Now a fashionably hirsute 13, **JOHN F. KENNEDY JR.** was a Manhattan eighth-grader who spent many a Tuesday afternoon in Central Park trying, with modest success, to better his tennis game.

BILL RAY

VIRGINIA JOHNSON, 49, and **WILLIAM MASTERS,** 58, drew on data from their St. Louis sex therapy clinic to tell, by way of tomes like *Human Sexual Response,* who was doing what with whom. Married in 1971 (her fourth, his second), they filed for divorce in 1992 but continued to collaborate professionally.

JILL KREMENTZ

At Carnegie Hall in her native Manhattan, an emotional stop on her three-continent farewell tour, diva **MARIA CALLAS** basked in her audience's bravas. Having lost Greek shipping tycoon Aristotle Onassis, her longtime love, to Jacqueline Bouvier Kennedy, Callas retired at 50; she died of a heart attack three years later.

HENRY GROSSMAN

BRUCE SPRINGSTEEN's first two LPs—*Greetings from Asbury Park* and *The Wild, the Innocent and the E-Street Shuffle*—won him more critical raves than sales. But the blue-collar rocker from the Jersey Shore, 24, was about to break out with a new song that would become not only his signature, but also the title cut of his next LP: "Born to Run."

DAVID GAHR

Disinherited by her father, 24-year-old **PALOMA PICASSO**—the daughter of Pablo Picasso and Françoise Gilot, the artist's longtime mistress—supported herself by designing costume jewelry. Until, that is, a French court ruled that though illegitimate, she and her brother Claude were entitled to share in dad's $100 million estate.

MARIO GIANCARLO BOTTI / SYGMA

Cinemagician **ALFRED HITCHCOCK** received both his first Oscar (an honorary award) and the attention of a fellow master of the plastic arts, Pop painter **ANDY WARHOL.** Hitchcock made one more movie (*Family Plot,* his 53rd) before his death at 81, in 1980; Warhol died in 1987, at 58, while hospitalized for routine gallbladder surgery.

JILL KREMENTZ

The legs of pro football quarterback **JOE NAMATH,** 31, were famous mainly for their fragility until he bared them for a panty-hose ad. But then, modesty never afflicted the superb athlete who, before Super Bowl III in 1969, had openly boasted that his New York Jets would whip the prohibitively favored Baltimore Colts (which they did, 16-7).

HARRY BENSON

Those proclaiming C&W as all washed up weren't listening to **DOLLY PARTON.** At 29, the pint-size singer parlayed her shimmering soprano and her outsize, er, bouffant into three No. 1 singles. Firmly en route to the throne as queen of country, this farmer's daughter from Locust Ridge, Tennessee, already had a palace—her 23-room spread in Nashville.

SLICK LAWSON

1975

To constitutionally protect women against gender-based discrimination, 1972's Equal Rights Amendment had seven years to win ratification by 38 states. Its most visible foe: lobbyist **PHYLLIS SCHLAFLY,** 50, of Alton, Illinois, who listed her occupation as "Mother." Though Congress extended the deadline, ERA was still three states shy when the clock ran out in June, 1982.

MICHAEL MAUNEY

Visiting Paris with cousin Maria Shriver, **CAROLINE KENNEDY,** 17, fell victim to a local lensman—and took matters into her own feet. (Mom Jacqueline Kennedy Onassis devised a more elegant safeguard to the family's privacy: a court order keeping one relentless New York paparazzo at least 25 feet from her and 30 feet from her children.)

ALEXANDRE / BARTHELEMY / GAMMA-LIAISON

This just in . . . Generalissimo Francisco Franco is still dead." Chevy Chase's sardonic weekend updates of the Spanish dictator's immutable condition help NBC's fledgling *Saturday Night Live* find an audience, as do the antics of such heretofore unknown resident troupers as John Belushi, Gilda Radner, Dan Aykroyd and Jane Curtin. Unlike the death of Franco, delayed for six weeks by extraordinary medical measures, those of three other perdurable autocrats were not. Haile Selassie, 82, the Lion of Judah, had been Ethiopia's Emperor for 58 years before being deposed the previous year. Chiang Kai-shek, 87, ruled the Republic of China for 25 years from the island redoubt of Taiwan, to which he had fled on losing the Mainland to Mao Tse-tung. And King Faisal, sovereign of Saudi Arabia for 11 years, is shot dead at 70 by a crazed nephew. In California, guns are also drawn against President Jerry Ford by Lynette "Squeaky" Fromme, 26, a disciple of mass murderer Charles Manson (she did not pull the trigger) and Sarah Moore, 45, a self-styled activist (she fired two rounds but missed).

The United States at last heeds the advice given in 1966 by George Aiken, the late Senator from Vermont, on ending its draining military presence in Vietnam: "Just declare victory and get out." At 7:52 p.m. on April 30, a CH-46 Sea Knight helicopter laden with 11 Marines struggles skyward from the roof of the American Embassy in Saigon, and the withdrawal is complete. Within 17 hours, North Vietnamese troops enter the capital, which is renamed Ho Chi Minh City.

Back home, network programming seems run by the Clone Ranger. Five of Nielsen's top seven series are spinoffs: *Laverne & Shirley* (from *Happy Days*), *Maude* (from *All in the Family*), *The Bionic Woman* (from *The Six Million Dollar Man*) and *Phyllis* and *Rhoda* (from *The Mary Tyler Moore Show*).

Passages: Political scientist-writer Hannah Arendt, 69. Former Teamsters Union head Jimmy Hoffa, 62 (who, after lunching at the Red Fox Inn in suburban Detroit and driving off in his dark green Pontiac, is never seen again). Ross McWhirter, 50 (who cofounded, with brother Norris, *The Guinness Book of World Records* to settle barroom wagers). Sitcom patriarch Ozzie Nelson, 69. Aristotle Onassis, 69. Cosmetics tycoon Charles Revson, 68. *Twilight Zone* creator Rod Serling, 50. Playwright Thornton (*Our Town*) Wilder, 78. Moviemaker William Wellman, 79 (whose 1927 *Wings* won the first Best Picture Oscar).

On the High Frontier, *Apollo* astronauts Thomas Stafford, Vance Brand and Deke Slayton and *Soyuz* cosmonauts Alexei Leonov and Valery Kubasov rendezvous their spacecrafts, mate airlocks and pay one another courtesy calls 140 miles above Earth. On the Electronic Frontier, Reed College drop-out Steve Jobs, 20, and pal Stephen Wozniak, 22, can be found in the Jobses' garage in Los Altos, California, wiring together the first commercial single-board computer with built-in ROM (read-only memory). The Apple I, bundled with its own software, would go on sale the next year for $666. IBM, also readying a personal computer for market, is letting others write software programs. So after just two years at Harvard, Bill Gates, 20, returns home to Seattle to work with friend Paul Allen, 22, on MS-DOS, a protocol to ensure that all the word-processing programs, spreadsheets, games et al., under development will be PC-compatible.

En route by chopper to yet another stop on his marathon shuttle between Israel and Egypt, **HENRY KISSINGER,** 52, and **NANCY MAGINNES KISSINGER,** 41, found a rare moment of Mideast peace. The second Mrs. K. was undoubtedly the only person permitted to openly address the famously gruff Secretary of State as "Sweetie."

DAVID RUBINGER

MICHAEL NICKLAUS had an excuse for the whiff; the club was a tad long for a 2-year-old. But not for dad **JACK,** who had already secured his place as the greatest golfer ever with 57 wins, including 15 majors, by age 35. Nor did he stop there; Nicklaus was to capture four more Grand Slam events, including the Masters when he was 46.

CO RENTMEESTER

The new First Family's liveliness could raise eyebrows, as when **BIANCA JAGGER,** 30, still the wife of Rolling Stone Mick, visited **JACK FORD** at the White House and nailed him with a Polaroid—not to mention when Jack, 23, admitted to having smoked pot.

DIRCK HALSTEAD

She may have been a pin-up girl in her *Barbarella* days and an antiwar activist reviled as "Hanoi Hannah" during the Vietnam era. But with second husband Tom Hayden, 35, running (in vain) for the U.S. Senate, it fell to **JANE FONDA,** 37, to push the shopping cart with kids **VANESSA VADIM,** 6 (by French director Roger), and **TROY GARITY,** 2 (by Hayden), in tow.

MICHAEL DOBO

VANGUARD
VANGUARD
VANGUARD

Having failed eight months earlier to jump from one rim of Idaho's Snake River Canyon to the other aboard a rocket-powered motorcycle, daredevil **EVEL KNIEVEL** thought a row of 13 double-decker buses at Wembley Stadium in London would be Harley heaven. Until, that is, his 750-cc. bike landed askew. Never again, vowed the mildly injured Kneivel, 36. But reports of his retirement proved premature.

DARBY HARPER / UPI / BETTMAN

Top billing went to Roy Scheider, Robert Shaw and Richard Dreyfuss; but then, they had agents. Not so the true star of *Jaws:* **BRUCE,** the mechanical Great White that director Steven Spielberg commissioned for the movie that packed the theaters even as it cleared the beaches.

LEWIS GOLDMAN / UNIVERSAL

Why did Chicago Mayor Richard Daley proclaim an official "Day" for **ANN-MARGRET,** 33? Perhaps because the Swedish-born star grew up in a suburb of the Windy City. Perhaps to mark her full recovery from the brutal 1972 fall, suffered on the stage of a Lake Tahoe casino, that left her comatose, with fractures of the jaw and five facial bones. Or perhaps Hizzoner was merely angling for first-night freebies to her latest movie, *Tommy.*

HENRY GROSSMAN

ELVIS PRESLEY turned (gasp!) 40, explaining perhaps why his act was now less lean-and-mean rock than bloated lounge. The King communed with his subjects via concerts in almost three dozen cities, but otherwise remained secluded behind the walls of Graceland, leaving it to loyalists to deny rumors that he was fond of alcohol and drugs.

STARFILE

A vice was perpetrated not in Miami, but in Hollywood, when **DON JOHNSON** began his affair with **MELANIE GRIFFITH** four years earlier; he was then 22, she only 14. The two actors married in 1976, divorced less than two years later (long before his hit network series), and remarried in 1989 (after her success in *Working Girl*).

MARY ELLEN MARK

BOB MACKIE, 34 (*left*), and **RAY AGHAYAN** were bosom buddies with the stars they costumed. Their hours could be crewel; a client like Cher, headliner of a weekly TV variety show since mid-1971, went through some 200 creations a year. But for keeping treadle to the metal, the partners sewed up fees as flamboyant as their designs: up to $1,500 per.

STEVE SCHAPIRO / GAMMA-LIAISON

Nine years after a near-fatal motorcycle crash and 18 months after a rocky comeback tour, America's most influential (and private) musicmaker, 34, set out to barnstorm the kind of small venues in which he had first performed. But though **BOB DYLAN**'s passions and one-of-a-kind voice seemed to be intact, his Rolling Thunder Revue was not able to bring it all back home; the fans, they were a-changin'.

KEN REGAN / CAMERA 5

The Rev. **SUN MYUNG MOON,** 55, spoke no English, yet preached to full houses in America. His acolytes denied that they were brainwashed, yet agreed to arranged marriages that were conducted en masse. He lived modestly in South Korea, yet was said to be worth $15 million. In 1984 Moon was found guilty of tax evasion and served 12 months—during which time his Unification Church won certification by the IRS as a genuine religion.

HARRY BENSON

Kojak wannabes? Nope, just female members of an Oakland, California, drug rehab program in a show of support for the close shave that was the group's sign of penance. **SYNANON,** founded in 1958, would spread to two continents, but had to retrench in 1980 when leader Chuck Dederich and two members were convicted of conspiring to commit murder. Their target: a lawyer who had sued the organization. Their weapon: a rattlesnake in his mailbox.

UPI / BETTMAN

When ex-stockbroker **JOSH REYNOLDS,** 33, found that certain crystals change color in response to minute temperature variations, he turned them into rings said to flag the mood of its wearers. Thus black meant hassled; light blue denoted tranquillity; and violet proclaimed ecstasy—or a hand too near the stove. One thing for sure: With 40 million rings sold in the first three months alone (at $45 to $250 the copy), the emotional state of other entrepreneurs was green (as with envy).

JOHN OLSON

1976

On September 22, 1976, *Charlie's Angels* ushered in the era of "jiggle TV." The hit ABC series about a trio of curvaceous private eyes initially starred (from left) **JACLYN SMITH,** 29, as The Shy One; **FARRAH FAWCETT-MAJORS,** 29, as The Braless One; and **KATE JACKSON,** 27, as The Smart One. Only Smith and **DAVID DOYLE,** 46, the Angels' liaison with the never-seen "Charlie," survived the show's entire six-year run.

JULIAN WASSER

Bicentennial Fever runs rampant in America. Centerpiece of the sea-to-shining-sea fête: an Independence Day parade up New York's Hudson River by 15 "tall ships," as well as 200-plus smaller vessels from 31 nations. Freedom of another sort had been spectacularly attained a day earlier in the Central African nation of Uganda, to which an Air France 727 had been skyjacked. With the tacit support of Ugandan dictator Idi Dada Amin, Arab, Palestinian and German terrorists demand in exchange for the passengers the release of 53 Palestinian and pro-Palestinian prisoners from Israeli jails. Israel answers by flying in special-forces commandos to stage a daring nighttime raid on the airport at Entebbe; 104 of the 105 hostages are rescued unharmed.

Within nine months, the People's Republic of China is rocked by the loss of its urbane Premier, Chou En-lai, 78, and its Great Helmsman, Mao Tse-tung, 82, and by one of history's most lethal earthquakes, which kills 242,000 in Tangshan, or a fourth of that city's population. (Another temblor, in Guatemala, claims 23,000 lives.) Not all massacres owe to Nature. South African security forces storm the black township of Soweto, leaving 100-plus residents dead.

Equal Rights Amendment or no, some women are doing just fine, thank you. Barbara Walters, 44, accepts network news' first $1 million-a-year salary to leave NBC after 12 seasons and co-anchor ABC's nightly national newscast with Harry Reasoner. The first female cadets are admitted to the Air Force Academy (155), Annapolis (81) and West Point (119). Ice-skater Dorothy Hamill wins Olympic gold at Innsbruck and makes short hair fashionable again. Sissy Spacek becomes a box-office force with a frightful turn in *Carrie* and Louise Lasser becomes a TV star with a ditzy turn in *Mary Hartman, Mary Hartman.*

What about the guys? Well, Jimmy Carter of Plains, Georgia, is elected the 39th President of the United States, and Robert MacNeil and James Lehrer start a low-budget PBS news show pronounced by critics as too unhip to survive.

Passages: Twenty-nine American Legionnaires convening at Philadelphia's Bellevue Stratford hotel (of an airborne bacterium, later named *Legionella pneumophila,* emanating from a dirty air-conditioning filter). Hollywood dance-meister Busby Berkeley, 80. Agatha Christie, 85. Eccentric billionaires J. Paul Getty, 83, and Howard Hughes, 70. Man of letters André Malraux, 75. Moviemaker Carol (*The Third Man, Oliver!*) Reed, 69. Leftist singer and black activist Paul Robeson, 77. Rosalind Russell, 63. Professional skier Vladimir "Spider" Sabich, 31 (shot dead by lover Claudine Longet, 34, ex-wife of singer Andy Williams).

Some 3,300 years after his burial, Tutankhamen is again walking like an Egyptian — or at least the funerary treasures of the XVII Dynasty king are, as part of an SRO seven-city tour that opens at Washington's National Gallery. The fabled Orient Express derails its Istanbul–Paris run after 144 years, but first-cabin travelers have a new toy. For $801, they can hop the supersonic Concorde at 10 a.m. in Europe and land at D.C.'s Dulles Airport at 8 a.m. (then down a second breakfast while waiting for customs and baggage). And 11 months and 450 million miles after launch, two NASA craft touch down on the Red Planet. Remote-operated probes detect the presence of water but not, alas, of Martian life.

Two years earlier she had been an entry-level TV newsreader in her hometown of Indianapolis. Then, as Chicago's first evening-news anchorwoman, she took flak for her blonde youthfulness and flat Hoosier accent. But JANE PAULEY, 25, laughed last; a week-long on-air audition won her a seat on NBC's *Today Show* replacing Barbara Walters, who had jumped to ABC for $1 million a year.

BOBBE WOLF

A peanut farmer for President? Well, JIMMY CARTER, 52, was also an ex-nuclear submariner and Georgia governor whose strength in the Deep South earned him the Democratic nomination over rivals like Morris Udall and Jerry Brown. Carter and Walter Mondale then captured enough support (though probably not that of this goober from Wrightsville, Georgia) to narrowly defeat the GOP ticket of Jerry Ford and Bob Dole.

UPI / BETTMAN

Decathlete **BRUCE JENNER,** 26, had banked on wife Chrystie's flight attendant salary to train for the Olympics; in Montreal, their sacrifice proved golden. Not so his stab at broadcasting, and in 1980, he left Chrystie for ex-Elvis flame Linda Thompson.

DAVID W. GIFFORD / SPORTS ILLUSTRATED

A gust of wind—rather than the sheer vehemence of his tell-it-like-it-is peroration—gave ABC sportscaster **HOWARD COSELL,** 56, a case of northern exposure. Perhaps that's why he kept his headphones on so firmly in the *Monday Night Football* booth.

MARGO CRABTREE

Pixyish Romanian gymnast **NADIA COMANECI,** 14, flashed an iron will while racking up three golds, one silver and one bronze at Montreal. But her reputation was badly tarnished by time. After the violent overthrow of Communist despot Nicolae Ceausescu—whose son Comaneci had romanced, post-Olympics—she fled to America in 1989 on the arm of an undivorced Romanian father of four.

ASSOCIATED PRESS

At sunset on the 2,400-acre Virginia estate of the man whom she had met six months earlier at a Washington, D.C., dinner, **ELIZABETH TAYLOR HILTON WILDING TODD FISHER BURTON BURTON,** 44, married **JOHN WARNER,** 49. A former Secretary of the Navy, Warner won election to the U.S. Senate in 1979, three years before the couple's divorce.

SUSAN McELHINNEY

BOB MARLEY popularized dreadlocks, *ganja* (or marijuana, a substance sanctioned by the Rastafarian sect to which he belonged) and, above all, the Afro-Caribe rhythms of reggae. The Jamaican singer died of brain cancer in 1981, at 36, with the knowledge that his song "I Shot the Sheriff" had topped the U.S. charts (albeit in a cover version by Eric Clapton).

DAVID BURNETT / CONTACT

A struggling actor named **SYLVESTER STALLONE** returned to Manhattan and his native Hell's Kitchen on the eve of a career-defining gamble. Having spurned $285,000 for a script he had written as a vehicle for himself, Stallone, 30, packaged both it and his acting services for $23,000 plus —yo!—10 percent of the net profits of *Rocky*.

KEN REGAN / CAMERA 5

Dueling yo-yos: Three years after their *Laugh-In* yukfest became Nielsen history, co-hosts **DAN ROWAN** (*left*) and **DICK MARTIN** reteamed for a PEOPLE tribute to the U.S. Bicentennial. Dan, 54, posed as Aaron Burr and Dick, 53, as Alexander Hamilton (whose fate not even a fickle finger could forestall; fancy that!).

STEVE SCHAPIRO

No, the gallows humor wasn't prompted by **SONNY BONO**'s divorce from Cher two years earlier. The singer, 36, was only impersonating doomed Revolutionary War hero Nathan Hale.

STANLEY TRETICK

Had network anchorman **JOHN CHANCELLOR,** 48, been as rewrite-happy as Thomas Jefferson, author of the Declaration of Independence, his NBC *Nightly News* would have aired the following morning—maybe.

ARTHUR SCHATZ

DIANE VON FURSTENBERG, at 29 already a successful fashion designer, slipped into something a little more Colonial to portray Philadelphia seamstress Betsy Ross, who had been 25 when she ran up the first Stars and Stripes.

HARRY BENSON

In PEOPLE' s recasting of history, England's George III turned out to be a reel do-little: British actor **REX HARRISON,** 68, sat as the monarch whose reign was plainly on the wane.

TERENCE SPENCER

The academic credentials of **SHERE HITE,** 34, were a little iffy (despite a master's in the social sciences, she had chosen to support herself for four years as a model). So too was her methodology (respondents to her self-devised questionnaire were not scientifically selected). No matter: *The Hite Report,* her compendium of 3,000 women's unexpurgated views on sex, was a runaway best-seller.

ARTHUR SCHATZ

Eight years before The Terminator introduced his trademark sneer—"I'll be back"—**ARNOLD SCHWARZENEGGER,** 28, was a champion iron-pumper flexing his dorsals (among other things) at the Whitney Museum in Manhattan. The self-styled Austrian Oak took part in an exhibit titled "Articulate Muscle." Among the rapt fans: **CANDICE BERGEN** (front left, with camera).

CO RENTMEESTER

TRUMAN CAPOTE, 51, was again biting the hand that fed him. A decade after *In Cold Blood,* his landmark "nonfiction novel," he seemed to relish guest shots on talk shows more than finishing his long-awaited roman à clef about the jet set. But this time, by publishing three bitchy segments as short stories, Capote so alienated society cronies that most snubbed him until his death, in 1984, of liver disease complicated by alcohol and drugs.

HARRY BENSON

The disco scene of thumping music, drugs and dance summitted in Manhattan's famed Studio 54. That was certainly the place to be spotted on New Year's Eve for such disheveled glitterati as designer **HALSTON** (*above);* **BIANCA JAGGER** and **ANDY WARHOL** *(right);* and **LIZA MINNELLI** and then husband **JACK HALEY JR.** (*top right).*

ROBIN PLATZER / TWIN IMAGES

1977

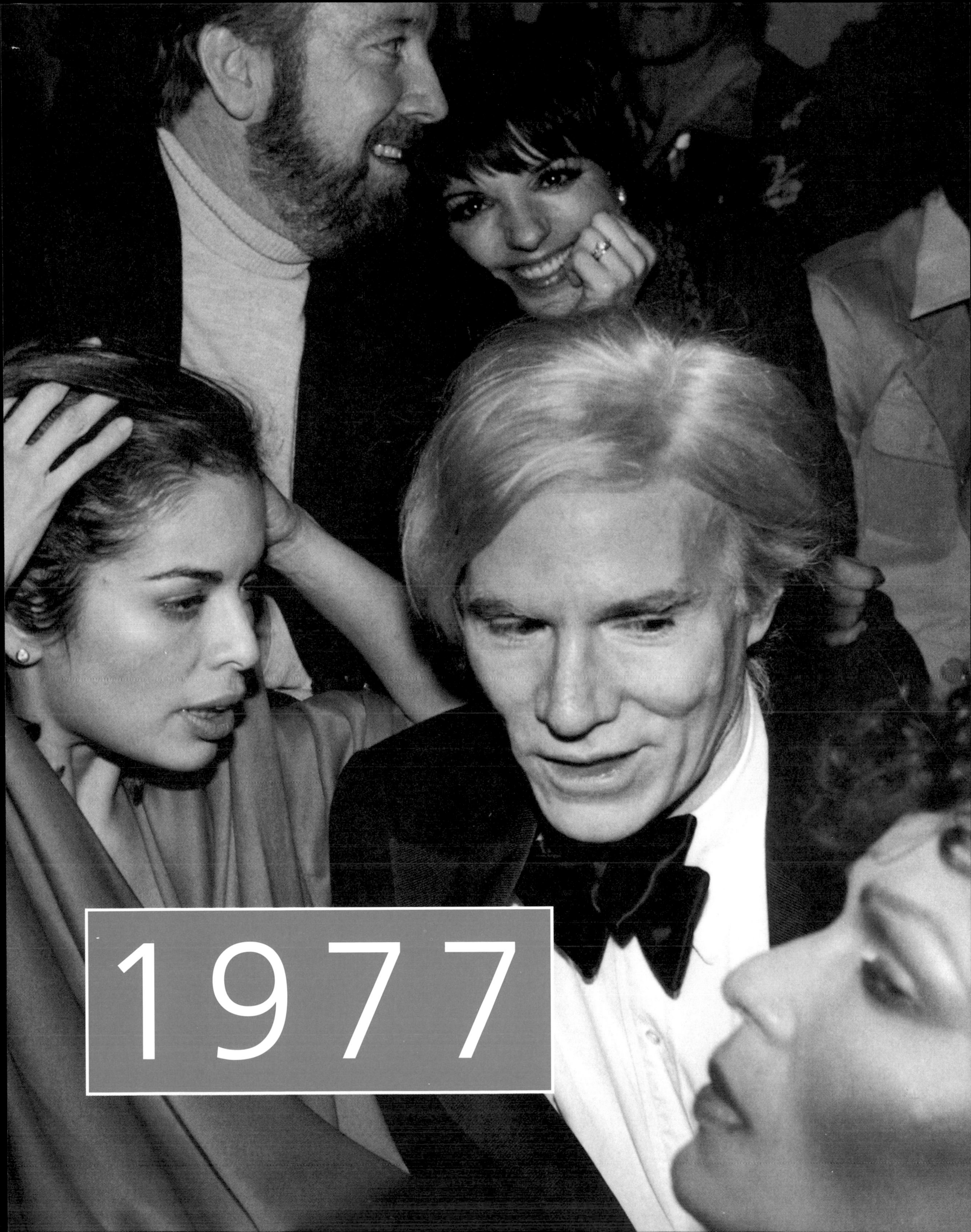

Stung by accusations that *Roots*, his epic testament to African-American history, was inaccurate and also pilfered in part, **ALEX HALEY** sought solace with a trip back to Juffure, his ancestral village in Gambia. The 55-year-old author (who later settled two plagiarism suits out of court) would publish only one more book before his death, of cardiac arrest, in 1992.

MICHAEL MAUNEY

He licensed his name to the brewers of Billy Beer and he would grace any tacky event anteing up his $5,000 fee, but **BILLY CARTER** wasn't just heavy—he was also our First Brother. Billy died of cancer of the pancreas in 1988, at 51.

JAY LEVITON

Dieting was in vogue, though not with twin pro wrestlers **BILLY** (*left*) and **BENNY McGUIRE,** 31, who weighed 1,474 pounds. Nowhere was their girth more prized, they reported, than Japan, a recent vacation stop. Sounds like a case of *cogito ergo sumo.*

DALE WITTNER

Kunta Kinte's cruel passage out of Africa hooks so many viewers in the opening hours of *Roots* that the nine-hour miniseries of the 1976 Alex Haley best-seller becomes the most watched TV show to date. Half of America tunes in the final night to learn the fate of Kunta's great-grandson Tom. Only one nagging question mars the ebullience at ABC: Why had the network scheduled the saga in January and not during a ratings-sweep month?

It is a good year for the Dream Factory, which even manages to upstage NASA. In April, the recyclable orbiter moves a big step closer to reality with the successful test flight of America's first shuttle, christened the *Enterprise* after *Star Trek*'s stately interstellar buggy. But by Memorial Day, the $2.5 billion space program seems as passé as the beam-me-up adventures of Kirk, Spock and crew; moviegoers are hurtling toward Darth Vader's Death Star alongside the valiant *Star Warriors,* a mesmeric illusion realized by 33-year-old George Lucas on a meager $8 million budget. Following closely is the ultimate chariot of fire, the Mother Ship of Steven Spielberg's *Close Encounters of the Third Kind.* And Hollywood, whose notions of charity can be suspect, lends a genuine hand to thrift shops by way of *Annie Hall*. Quicker'n you can say "la-di-dah," Diane Keaton wannabes are scouring Salvation Army and Goodwill outlets for baggy hand-me-downs. (Boys of all ages, meanwhile, are scouring stores for the glossy 20" x 28", $2 poster of the toothsome Farrah Fawcett-Majors, which sells more than 5 million copies to become the most popular wall decoration ever.)

In a year when President Jimmy Carter calls belt-tightening at the self-pump line "the moral equivalent of war," Johnny Paycheck captures the dour national mood (and crosses over from C&W) with the hit "Take This Job and Shove It." Japanese baseball legend Sadaharu Oh, 37, is too polite to tell newly retired Henry Aaron to do likewise with the all-time home-run record; the Taiwan-born slugger just goes out and blasts an unprecedented 756th Kirin Klout.

Passages: South African antiapartheid activist Steven Biko, 38 (while in police detention). Charlie Chaplin, 88. Joan Crawford, 69 (mercifully, 18 months before the publication of adopted daughter Christina Crawford's best-selling tell-all, *Mommie Dearest*). Bing Crosby, 73. Novelist James (*From Here to Eternity*) Jones, 55. Peter Goldmark, 71 (inventor, in 1948, of the long-playing 33⅓ rpm album). Musicmaker (and traditional New Year welcomer) Guy Lombardo, 75. Marx Brothers Gummo, 84, and Groucho, 86. Vladimir Nabokov, 78. Erotic memoirist Anaïs Nin, 73. Onetime CIA pilot Francis Gary Powers, 47 (whose capture in 1960, after his U-2 spy plane was shot down over the USSR, led to the cancellation of a superpower summit between Dwight Eisenhower and Nikita Khruschev). Sitcom star Freddie Prinze, 22 (a suicide).

Among the 135 freshmen entering the University of Michigan in January is an 18-year-old scholarship student whose ID card reads: Ciccone, Madonna Louise. Australia, like Hollywood, makes surfing epics too, so Mel Gibson, 21, wins his first movie role in *Crazy Summer.* And though Columbia Pictures head David Begelman earns $234,000 a year, he is also forging checks, a habit that will end when actor Cliff Robertson scans his bank statement and calls the police.

The Jacksons had recently quit Motown Records (in the process dropping the "Five" from their name). But though **MICHAEL,** 18, was still singing with brothers Tito, Jackie, Jermaine and Marlon, he preferred to hang out with sister **JANET,** 11.

RON GALELLA

Do Ya Think I'm Alpo? Going Hollywood seemed to agree with Scottish rocker **ROD STEWART,** 30, and best friend King: The raspy-voiced vocalist had a new live-in love, actress **BRITT EKLAND,** 34, and a new single, "Tonight's the Night (Gonna Be Alright)," his first chart-topper since 1971's "Maggie May."

STEVE SCHAPIRO

Bagel the beagle found his master's voice utterly inescapable. As did we all: **BARRY MANILOW,** 31, warbled not only the high-rotation jingles of Dr Pepper and McDonald's ("You Deserve a Break Today"), but also the monster hit "I Write the Songs" (written in fact by Bruce Johnston and first recorded by The Captain and Tennille and then by David Cassidy).

STEVE SCHAPIRO

George Lucas's *Star Wars* was a tribute to Japanese director Akira Kurosawa's *The Hidden Fortress,* but what in the far-off heavens inspired **C3PO** (*left*) and **R2D2**? Not about to ask were British actors **ANTHONY DANIELS,** 31 (*standing*), and **KENNY BAKER,** 42 (*steering*), who were only too glad that The Force would remain with them through a pair of sequels.

LUCASFILM LTD (ABOVE); TERENCE SPENCER

The King is dead—long live the instant memorabilia (as well as the equally schlocky impersonators). At 3:30 p.m. on August 16, 1977, after 17 No. 1 singles, one failed marriage and one 9-year-old daughter, **ELVIS ARON PRESLEY** died in Memphis, Tennessee, at age 42, of what was officially listed as "cardiac arrhythmia."

CO RENTMEESTER

Why shouldn't these feet be happy? So what if their owner was making a criminally low $500-a-week paycheck; the post-prime-time exposure that **GILDA RADNER** got each Saturday night, live, was priceless. (Check the bookcase for a mugshot of the funny lady we also knew as Baba Wawa, Lisa Lubner and Emily ["Never mind"] Litella.) Radner was 42 when she died of ovarian cancer in 1989.

HARRY BENSON

In the finale of his 160th ballet, *Vienna Waltzes,* 50 dancers swirled across the stage—and imperious choreographer **GEORGE BALANCHINE,** 73, made sure each got it right. So secure was the Russian emigré of his New York City Ballet's reputation that he rejected the job applications of defecting superstars Rudolf Nureyev and Mikhail Baryshnikov. Balanchine worked right up to his death in 1983.

MARTHA SWOPE

Trimming off 25 of the pounds that made him *Welcome Back, Kotter*'s cuddliest Sweathog, **JOHN TRAVOLTA,** 23, strutted to big-screen stardom in *Saturday Night Fever* as the disco champ from Brooklyn who harbors dreams of conquering Manhattan (and dancing partner **KAREN GORNEY**).

MARTHA SWOPE

Under tight security while awaiting trial in Colorado for killing a nurse, **TED BUNDY,** 31, still escaped his Aspen jail cell. He was recaptured in Florida the next year and charged with three fresh murders (of two college sorority sisters and a junior high school girl). Convicted, the clean-cut serial killer professed innocence right up until his execution in 1989. Authorities, though, believed that Bundy had brutally slain at least 22 women in five states.

JERRY GAY

Sharecropper's son **LARRY FLYNT,** 34, and fourth wife **ALTHEA LEASURE,** 23, turned a go-go club newsletter into the ultra-raunchy—and ultra-profitable—skin mag *Hustler.* The next year Flynt, on trial for obscenity in Georgia, was shot by an avowed racist and left a paraplegic. In 1987 Leasure, who had AIDS-related complex, apparently drowned in the tub at the couple's home in Los Angeles.

GORDON BAER

He wasn't exactly Mr. Mom, but **TED KOPPEL,** 36, took a one-year leave from his correspondent's job at ABC News so wife **GRACE ANNE** could concentrate on her first year of law school rather than their four children. In 1980 she passed the bar and entered practice in Virginia; by then, he had begun anchoring late-night updates of the embassy hostage crisis in Iran, a daily feature that grew into *Nightline.*

DON CARL STEFFEN

Having made her mark on movies by baring skin, **BRIGITTE BARDOT** hoped to make a mark on the ecosystem by saving skins like that of this baby seal. The actress, semi-retired at 42, flew to Newfoundland to protest the annual Canadian harvest of harp seals. But reporters proved hostile (one accused Bardot of wearing fur) and hunters proceeded to bag some 175,000 pelts.

MIROSLAV BROZEK / SYGMA

A dozen years after swatting her first tennis ball, **TRACY AUSTIN** was playing the hallowed courts of Wimbledon. The tournament's youngest invitee ever—at 14, she still adored the exploits of Nancy Drew and the Fonz—won two matches before being eliminated. Austin captured the U.S. Open in 1979, but her promise went sadly unfulfilled because of a series of major injuries.

CO RENTMEESTER

At 38, Alabama's First Lady, **CORNELIA WALLACE,** could still execute the stunts that had made her a Cypress Gardens headliner in the early '60s. Not so stable was her six-year marriage to Governor George Wallace, 58, who filed for divorce later in the year.

© 1993 FLORIDA CYPRESS GARDENS INC.

SUZANNE SOMERS had been just a pretty face in 1973's *American Graffiti* (she portrayed the iconic blonde in the white T-Bird). Some of her other talents were showcased when the 29-year-old actress won a role on the smash ABC sitcom *Three's Company.* She quit the series in 1981 over a contract dispute; none of Somers's later network projects had quite the impact of her commercials promoting the exergizmo called the Thighmaster.

HARRY BENSON

1978

Stars of network flops rarely failed upward into big-screen stardom. Yet **BURT REYNOLDS**, 42, had managed to segue from low-Nielsen series like *Hawk* and *Dan August* into fare like *Smokey and the Bandit,* the grosses of which helped prompt theater owners to name him Star of the Year. Offscreen the actor, divorced from *Laugh-In*'s Judy ("Sock-It-to-Me") Carne and past his four-year liaison with Dinah Shore, was dating *Smokey* costar Sally Field.
HARRY BENSON

California's golden statehood is dimmed by two events. Onetime San Francisco city supervisor Dan White, 32, denied reappointment, takes his grudge and a .38-caliber revolver to City Hall, where he shoots dead avowedly gay supervisor Harvey Milk, 48, and Mayor George Moscone, 49 (who is succeeded by Dianne Feinstein, 44). The next year, White, in essence claiming that the Devil Dog made him do it, would be convicted only for voluntary manslaughter on grounds that his penchant for junk food had driven him temporarily insane. Of more far-reaching significance is a statewide referendum initiative championed most visibly by retired home-appliance manufacturer Howard Jarvis, 75. Proposition 13, passed in November, slashes property taxes 57 percent — and eventually compromises California's ability to deliver vital services like education.

Mohammad Reza Pahlavi's 37-year rule as the Shah of Iran hits a speed bump when a rash of strikes and demonstrations compels him to impose martial law. Fomenting the discord long-distance is an exiled Muslim cleric of the Shiite sect whose tape-recorded sermons are smuggled back home and played in Iran's mosques. But the Shah's security forces deem the Ayatollah Ruhollah Khomeini, 78, so inconsequential that he is allowed to live unharmed in a Paris suburb.

Eight years after the Beatles set off separately down "The Long and Winding Road" (their last No. 1 single), we say auf Weidersehen to the Beetle. Having turned out 21 million Bugs in 47 years in Germany, Volkswagen will henceforth manufacture the homely but economical car only in Brazil, Mexico and Nigeria. In Motor City news, Henry Ford II decides he really doesn't like the executive who in a 31-year career produced hits like the Mustang, so he fires Lee Iacocca.

Arriving at a theater near you: Hollywood's first big-budget Vietnam pictures since 1968's *The Green Berets* (in which John Wayne walked east into the sunset). According to Michael Cimino's *The Deer Hunter,* the Big Muddy was one long game of Russian roulette. According to Hal Ashby's *Coming Home,* it produced paraplegics who compensate by learning to become sensitive lovers.

King Hussein of Jordan, 42, takes as wife No. 2 Lisa Halaby of New York City, a 26-year-old Princeton graduate who becomes Queen Noor. And Christina Onassis, 27, heir to her late father Aristotle's shipping empire, takes as husband No. 3 Sergei Kauzov, a 37-year-old, one-eyed Muscovite with reputed KGB ties.

Passages: Ventriloquist Edgar Bergen, 75. Civil War historian Bruce (*A Stillness at Appomattox*) Catton, 78. Surrealist painter Giorgio de Chirico, 90. Mathematician Kurt Godel, 71. Anthropologist Margaret Mead, 76. Former Israeli Prime Minister (and Milwaukee native) Golda Meir, 80. Willy Messerschmitt, 80 (German aviation designer and manufacturer whose planes included the Luftwaffe's vaunted World War II fighters). Painter Norman Rockwell, 84. Boxer Gene Tunney, 80 (kayoed by Jack Dempsey in a 1927 title fight, he got a second chance when his opponent's failure to proceed immediately to a neutral corner resulted in the referee's infamous "long count").

Good news for travelers: The deregulation of U.S. airlines is billed as the prelude to lower fares and better service, promises that win the clear-skies endorsement of major carriers like — remember? — Eastern, Pan Am and Braniff.

JIM JONES's claims of bringing 43 believers back from the dead caught the attention of Bay Area authorities. He moved his Peoples Church to Guyana, but California Congressman Leo Ryan flew down to investigate. After "Jonestowners" killed Ryan and an aide, the faith healer, 47, told congregants to drink from a vat of cyanide-laced grape Fla-Vor-Aid. The 913 who obeyed—including, sadly, children and infants—passed beyond resurrection.

SAN FRANCISCO PROGRESS

MICHAEL LANDON had a prime-time winner in *Little House on the Prairie,* costarring (*from left*) **MELISSA GILBERT,** 14; Bandit; **KAREN GRASSLE,** 34 (holding little **WENDY TURNEBEAUGH**); **MELISSA SUE ANDERSON,** 15; and **LINDSAY GREENBUSH,** 7. Landon, who also achieved hits in the '60s (*Bonanza*) and '80s (*Highway to Heaven*), was prepping still another series when he died of cancer in 1991, at age 53.

NBC

DAKOTA

In just a Na Nu-second, **ROBIN WILLIAMS,** 26, leaped from obscure stand-up to network star by way of *Mork and Mindy,* on which he portrayed a naif from the planet Ork. It didn't hurt that, like *Laverne and Shirley* before it, the new series, which costarred Pam Dawber, was a spin-off of that ABC powerhouse, *Happy Days.*

WYNN MILLER

He was a self-styled suburban tough from Long Island who also used his dukes to pummel the ivories well enough to acquire the handle "Piano Man," after his first Top 25 single. At 28, **BILLY JOEL** released "Just the Way You Are," which fought its way to No. 3.

KEN REGAN / CAMERA 5

No one had more reason to play the crying game than **BILLY CRYSTAL**'s wife, Janice. Her husband of eight years, the father of their two daughters, managed to land a pair of breakthrough roles. But on the sitcom *Soap*, he was cast as prime-time's first overtly gay blade, and in Joan Rivers's *Rabbit Test,* he played history's first pregnant guy. No matter; Crystal, 31, managed to look simply *mah*-velous.

JIM McHUGH

BROOKE SHIELDS, 12, thought that a movie about a child prostitute, replete with a nude scene, was kind of weird—even though she played just that role in *Pretty Baby.* A model since the age of 11 months, she made six more pictures (most, like *Wanda Nevada, Tilt* and *Endless Love,* eminently forgettable) before enrolling at Princeton.

HARRY BENSON

Thousand-dollar-a-day model **JERRY HALL** of Mesquite, Texas, would have turned heads even without her yearlong affair with Mick Jagger (then still wed to Bianca). At the time, Hall, 21, professed no desire to marry the head Stone. But 12 years later, with their daughter and son in attendance, she became the second Mrs. J.

HARRY BENSON

It was a risqué pose for Canada's First Lady, but then **MARGARET TRUDEAU,** 29, had just left Prime Minister Pierre Trudeau, 58, after seven years and three sons. He lost his office the next year but soon won a third term; though seen squiring dates like Barbra Streisand, he remained single. Maggie had a fling at acting before remarrying in 1984.

OSCAR ABOLAFIA

Priced from $49.95 down to $10 per, skateboards were a natural choice for those too cash-impaired (or simply too young) to flaunt a hot rod. The polyurethane-wheeled planks also enriched the medical profession, which reported treating some 335,000 injuries a year suffered by novices trying to emulate the gravity-nullifying moves of pros like 20-year-old TONY ("MAD DOG") ALVA.

JOHN ZIMMERMAN

Few would buy a how-to book on walking, so why was *The Complete Book of Running* a shoe-in for the year's best-selling title? Perhaps because 650,000 health-conscious Americans alone (the book was also published in 14 other countries) sensed the benefits of roadwork. Chief among them: author **JIM FIXX,** a magazine editor who shed 60 pounds after taking up the sport. Yet he died six years later, at 52, of a heart attack—suffered while running.

KEN REGAN / CAMERA 5

First Daughter **AMY CARTER,** 11, played to a captive house aboard Air Force One: Mom **ROSALYNN;** Mrs. Carter's press secretary, **MARY HOYT;** White House chief of staff **HAMILTON JORDAN** (*left*); and White House press secretary **JODY POWELL.** Amy's dad, in the second year of his presidency, produced sweet music of his own by inviting Israel's Menachim Begin and Egypt's Anwar Sadat to Camp David and orchestrating a Mideast peace agreement.

KARL SCHUMACHER / THE WHITE HOUSE

JOHN F. KENNEDY JR. was 17 and still a year away from enrolling at Brown University when he dropped in on the RFK tennis tourney, an annual celebrity benefit in New York City. (It was at the 1977 bash that his cousin, Maria Shriver, first met her future husband, Arnold Schwarzenegger.)

RON GALELLA

The Roman Catholic Church's third Supreme Pontiff in two months, and the first non-Italian elected by the College of Cardinals since the 16th Century, **JOHN PAUL II,** 68, was born Karol Wojtyla in Krakow, Poland. He succeeded Paul VI, who died at 80 after a papacy of 15 years, and John Paul I, 65, who died only 34 days after his installation.

CONTRASTO / SABA

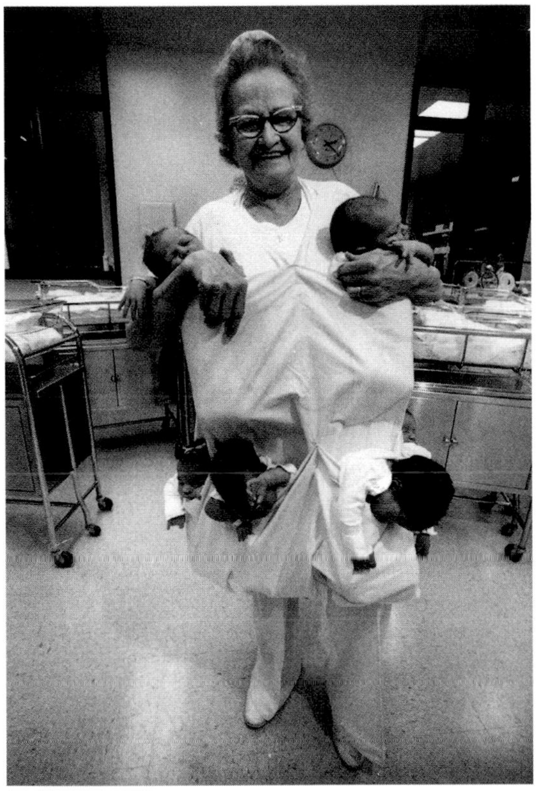

During three decades as a pediatrics ward nurse, **VERA LEONARD,** 69, of Greensboro, North Carolina, would find herself pondering the dire consequences if the hospital were struck by a disaster such as fire. Which was why she and sister Treva Ellis designed a patented "evacuation gown" (confirming the adage that sometimes, all kids need a good smock).

WILL McINTYRE

Six years after arriving in Washington, D.C., as gifts from the People's Republic of China, **LING-LING** was still turning her back on **HSING-HSING**'s passes. National Zookeepers tried gambits that included slimming diets to make the pandas bare their passions. But Ling-Ling bore only four cubs (none of which lived beyond four days) before her death, at 23, in 1992.

SABIN ROBBINS / FRIENDS OF THE NATIONAL ZOO

Back when New York City was referred to (with envy) as "The Big Apple," there was better food, at cheaper prices, elsewhere. Yet no table was harder to book than one at the eponymous Upper East Side boite run by **ELAINE KAUFMAN.** Abrim with home-grown authors and actors, Left Coast drop-ins, rock demimondes and the stray jock (not to mention awed tourists), Elaine's was a nightly pot-au-feu of the vanities.

JILL KREMENTZ

If Jimmy Carter could schlep First Luggage on and off the First Boeing, then another good old boy could surely bag his own across the South Lawn. **WILLIE NELSON,** 45, even made it inside without being busted by the local constabulary. But then, he had been asked up from Texas to entertain a fast-track audience: a White Houseful of stock-car racing's best drivers.

TERRY ARTHUR

Was **OLIVIA NEWTON-JOHN** screen-testing for *Cujo?* No, the English-born, Australian-reared C&W star, 29, was just telling Domino—one unmelancholy Great Dane—that she now had a rock hit, too: "You're the One That I Want," her chart-topping duet with *Grease* costar John Travolta.

RICK SEIREENI

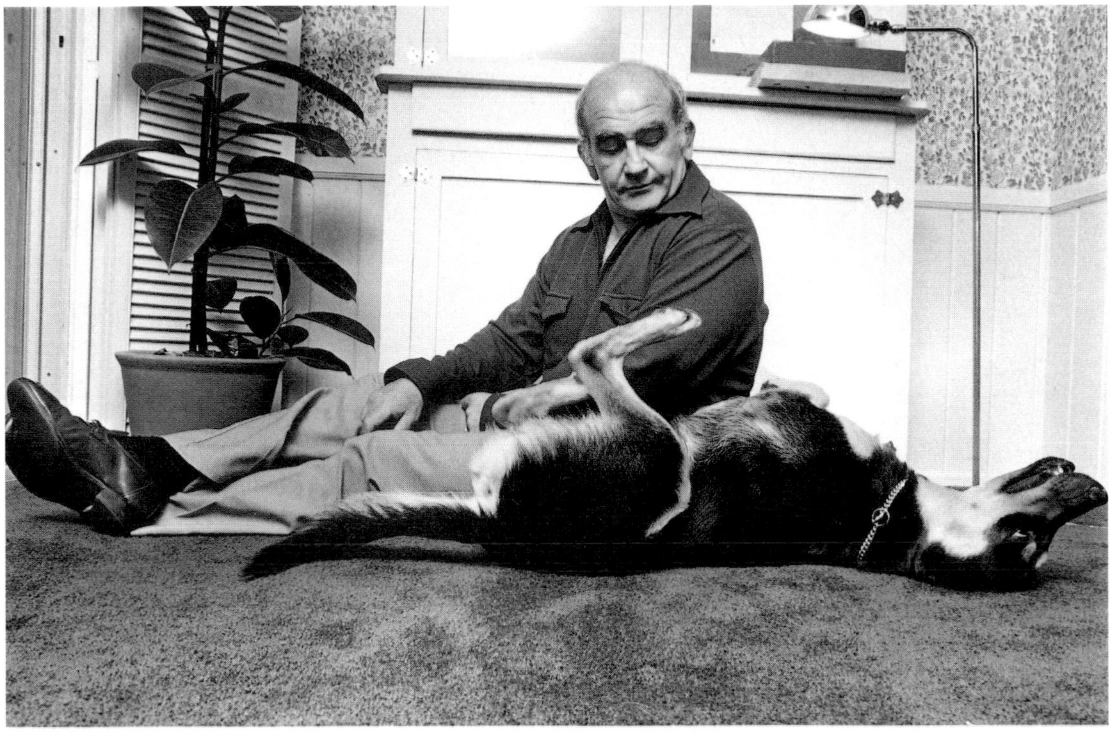

Even after winning a trio of Emmys during *The Mary Tyler Moore Show*'s seven-year run and two more for the miniseries *Rich Man, Poor Man* and *Roots,* **ED ASNER,** 48, seemed less impressed than pooch Gatsby about finally landing his own series, *Lou Grant.*

MARK SENNET

To a billion Chinese it was the Year of the Sheep—but then, what did they know from *The Muppet Show,* that small-screen fave, or *The Muppet Movie,* that big-screen rave? For the rest of us, it was truly an *annus porcinus* (sorry, Kermit). **MISS PIGGY**'s movie debut came a little late for the much-heralded Me Decade of the '70s. *C'a fait rien.* She turned the '80s into the *Moi* Decade.

NANCY MORAN

1979

Two of America's staunchest Cold War allies are deposed and, with their retinues, turned into bands on the run. The Shah of Iran, 59, had spent much of his nation's OPEC billions not only on modernizing his military but also unveiling the ways of the West to his Muslim nation. Offended Shiite fundamentalists drive him from the Peacock Throne and welcome back the exiled Ayatollah Khomeini. Nicaraguan President Anastasio Somoza Debayle, 53, treated the country's treasury as his own, as had his father and brother before him. The Sandinistas, leftist rebels led by Jesuit-schooled Daniel Ortega Saavedra, 33, force him to flee on a Learjet crammed with boxes of gold; Somoza would find refuge but not safety in Paraguay where, 14 months later, his car is bazookaed to bits.

In America, nuclear energy advocates scornfully dismiss as mere Hollywood fiction *The China Syndrome,* in which Jane Fonda uncovers safety violations at a power plant. Thirteen days after the picture's premiere, a failure in the cooling system of Reactor No. 2 at the Three Mile Island plant near Harrisburg, Pennsylvania, partially melts down the uranium core; the resulting radioactivity would take 14 years and $1 billion to clean up. Considerably less hot are the three networks' attempt to replicate the gross-out humor that had made *Animal House* the previous year's killer comedy. None of the frat-ratcoms lasts even a semester (the resident blonde bombshell of ABC's *Delta House,* though, emerges unscathed: 20-year-old Michelle Pfeiffer). But the old college rah-rah is in ample evidence on a new all-sports cable channel, ESPN, which pads out its initial 88-hour-a-week schedule with Slo-Pitch softball and midget car races.

The Nobel Prize for Peace is awarded to Agnes Gonxha Bojaxhiu, 69. Born to Albanian parents in what later became Yugoslavia, she emigrated to India at age 17, took a nun's vows and, in 1948, as Mother Teresa, founded the Missionaries of Charity. Two others with *The Right Stuff* (the title of Tom Wolfe's best-seller about America's first astronauts): Earvin "Magic" Johnson, who leads Michigan State to the NCAA basketball title over Larry Bird's Indiana State team.

Passages: Cartoonist Al (*L'il Abner*) Capp, 70. Bluegrass picker Lester Flatt, 64. Depression-era Public Enemy Alvin "Creepy" Karpis, 75. World War II hero and overseer of India and Pakistan's leave-taking from the British Empire, Earl Mountbatten, 79 (of an IRA bomb aboard his fishing boat). Merle Oberon, 68. Baseball owner Walter O'Malley, 75 (who in 1958 moved his Brooklyn Dodgers to L.A.). Silent-screen heroine Mary Pickford, 86. Fan dancer Sally Rand, 75. Popster Minnie (*Lovin' You*) Riperton, 31. Jean Seberg, 40. Bishop Fulton J. Sheen, 84 (whose weekly '50s inspirational TV series, *Life Is Worth Living,* was an improbable prime-time hit). Hollywood potentate Daryl F. Zanuck, 77 (a biography of whom was subtitled, *Don't Say Yes Until I Finish Talking*).

In December, the USSR sends troops into Afghanistan to suppress the Muslim insurgents threatening its client regime in Kabul. An anti-Soviet guerrilla force, the *mujahedin,* wins instant backing from the Muslim world and from the CIA, which openly arms it. Among the alliances forged is one between U.S. intelligence and a blind Egyptian sheik, Omar Abdel Rahman, who would in 1993 be charged with masterminding the bombing of the.World Trade Center.

With inflation topping 20 percent, British voters invited the Tories, led by MARGARET THATCHER, 54, to unsling their country's economic posterior. The nation's first woman Prime Minister parlayed political savvy and a rep for ruthlessness (one nickname: "Attila the Hen") into an 11-year residency at 10 Downing Street, the longest unbroken governance since the Earl of Liverpool's (1812-1827).

SRDJA DJUKANOVIC / THE DAILY TELEGRAPH / CAMERA PRESS

When ousted Ford president LEE IACOCCA, 55, took the top job at Chrysler, that automaker's future looked skeletal. But he won a $1.5 billion congressional bailout, cut costs and rolled out popular new models—all for $1 a year. There were, to be sure, long-term rewards: a treasure trove of company stock, plus royalties from a 1988 autobiography that sold almost 7 million copies.

CO RENTMEESTER

Certainly, Joan Rivers's mirth over **ELIZABETH TAYLOR**'s girth was cruel: "At SeaWorld, she saw Shamu leap out of the tank and asked, 'Does it come with potatoes?'" The actress, 47, had an excuse; husband John Warner's run for the U.S. Senate meant endless campaign noshing. Yet, as her arrival at Studio 54 with club owner **STEVE RUBELL** demonstrated, Taylor had grown into quite a ripe target.

KEN REGAN / CAMERA 5

Whoever said that it ain't over till the fat lady sings never sampled the drop-dead pasta sauce—four parts butter, one part blue cheese—that was tenor **LUCIANO PAVAROTTI**'s signature dish. Neither could the opera star, 43, after doctors, hoping to forestall an early trip to Valhalla, placed him on a 2,000-calories-a-day diet.

DAVID RUBINGER

GERMAINE GREER had trampled on the male establishment with her angry 1970 best-seller, *The Female Eunuch.* Now teaching at the University of Tulsa, the Cambridge-educated Australian feminist, 40, still toed no party line; she considered the proposed ERA to be legislative "whitewash."

SHELLY KATZ / BLACK STAR

MERYL STREEP's first major movie role was hardly sympathetic: Marching to the beat of her own (feminist) drummer, she deserts a husband and young son. But *Kramer v. Kramer* propelled the stage-trained actress, 30, into a heady Hollywood trajectory. Over the next decade and a half, she earned eight Oscar nominations—and won twice—even though she lived on the East Coast with her sculptor husband and their four kids.

THEO WESTENBERGER / GAMMA-LIAISON

While **CAROL BURNETT** and producer husband Joe Hamilton worked to keep her CBS comedy hour high in the Nielsens, daughter **CARRIE HAMILTON** was substance-abusing her way through junior high. Finally Burnett, born to alcoholic parents, sent Carrie, 14, to a Houston rehab center. The six-month treatment bore fruit; she later won a role on TV's *Fame* and in 1988 costarred not only in a theatrical, *Tokyo Pop,* but also the telemovie *Hostage*—opposite mom.

STEVE SCHAPIRO

The transparent bid for attention was no surprise: at 32, **CHER**'s second marriage, to Greg Allman, was history, as were her days as a Top 10 hitmaker and TV variety host. But the singer had an ace hidden somewhere, if not up her sleeve. Four years later, the movie *Silkwood* would launch a drama career that led her, by way of 1985's *Mask,* to the Best Actress Oscar for 1987's *Moonstruck*.

ROBIN PLATZER / TWIN IMAGES

Senator **JOHN TOWER** of Texas was mightier than a locomotive in championing the Defense Department and faster than a speeding bullet en route to D.C. parties. But his autocratic ways and fondness for alcohol would become post-retirement Kryptonite; in 1989 former colleagues rejected his nomination as George Bush's Secretary of Defense. Two years later, Tower, 64, was killed in a plane crash in Brunswick, Georgia.

DAVID WOO / DALLAS MORNING NEWS

One-trick phonies, scoffed critics of the Village People. The group—biker **GLENN HUGHES,** Indian chief **FELIPE ROSE,** cowboy **RANDY JONES,** cop **VICTOR WILLIS,** G.I. **ALEX BRILEY** and hardhat **DAVID HODO**—was too busy banking their "Y.M.C.A." royalties to care. Yet just as disco proved as ephemeral a fad as roller-skating, so the sextet's first mega-single was also their last.

RAEANNE RUBENSTEIN

MARVIN and **MARCELLA MITCHELSON** had been married 18 years, even though at 51, his L.A. law practice thrived on high-profile divorces (including two of Zsa-Zsa Gabor's). But in 1989 the man who pioneered "palimony"—awards to jilted live-ins—came under scrutiny for legal malpractice. And four years later, he drew a $2.1 million fine and a 30-month jail sentence after being found guilty of tax evasion.

TONY KORODY / SYGMA

Heir to one of America's great fortunes, **GLORIA VANDERBILT** was a survivor of woes out of a Judith Krantz potboiler. She had been the subject of an infamous 1930s custody battle, entered into three failed marriages and then been widowed. But at 55, the painter and commercial designer achieved a measure of happiness by fronting (or was it backing?) America's top-selling line of signature denims. You might call it a triumph of jean-ealogy.

EVELYN FLORET

The *Complete Scarsdale Medical Diet,* with its promise of revealing just why the rich are never too thin, made cardiologist **HERMAN TARNOWER** (who actually lived in the neighboring New York City suburb of Purchase) a best-selling author at 69. But the next year, he was shot dead by his 56-year-old paramour, girls' school headmistress Jean Harris, whom he had discarded for 37-year-old medical aide **LYNN TRYFOROS.**

ARTHUR SCHATZ

JOHN McENROE's left-handed serves and volleys were deadly. So was the tongue that he wielded to rile officials and hecklers alike. Six years younger than Jimmy Connors, whom he had dethroned as tennis's reigning hothead, McEnroe at 20 became the youngest man to win the U.S. Open, a title he would successfully defend until 1982.

SUSAN WEINIK

Even guys who were math-challenged could get to *10,* thanks to **BO DEREK,** 22, who had the title role —if not many lines of dialogue—in the hit Dudley Moore comedy of that name. But America's dewiest decimal seemed not to know diddley about career management, allowing husband John Derek, 52, to direct her in movies like 1981's *Tarzan, the Ape Man* and 1984's *Bolero;* their grosses were decidedly unbodacious.

PHOTOFEST

Unfazed by that fatal night at Chappaquiddick a decade earlier and by his separation from wife Joan, Senator **EDWARD KENNEDY,** 47, ran for President against incumbent (and fellow Democrat) Jimmy Carter. But the bid came unglued when, on national TV, he was unable to articulate his reason for seeking the White House. He and Joan were divorced in 1983.

MICHAEL ABRAMSON

The bride was **SUSAN FORD,** at 21 a freelance photographer, and the groom divorced Secret Service agent **CHARLES VANCE,** 37. Among their well-wishers were **JERRY FORD;** Vance's mother, **CHRISTINE EARLEY;** and **BETTY FORD.** The newlyweds, who had become acquainted during Vance's assignment to the Ford White House, had two children before their 1988 divorce; the next year, she married a lawyer from Oklahoma.

UPI / BETTMANN

Three years after Jimmy Carter commuted her sentence for armed robbery, **PATTY HEARST,** 25, was given away in marriage by dad **RANDOLPH** to San Francisco policeman **BERNARD SHAW,** 33. They had met on her second day of freedom; Shaw was among the off-duty cops hired to guard her. When he became a security consultant, the couple moved to Connecticut, where they began raising three children.

TONY KORODY / SYGMA

On November 4, after President Jimmy Carter allowed the deposed Shah of Iran to enter the U.S. for cancer treatments, Muslim revolutionaries loyal to the Ayatollah Khomeini overran Western legations in Tehran. Among the 53 prisoners seized at the American Embassy: attaché **BARRY ROSEN,** 34. (Two of the private citizens captured were rescued in a paramilitary operation financed by their boss, Texas tycoon Ross Perot.) Not even the Shah's death in Egypt nine months later appeased Khomeini; he would eventually free all the hostages, but not to Carter and not before they had spent 444 days in harrowing captivity.

LEDRU / SYGMA

1980

December 8 became another day the music died: **JOHN LENNON** was gunned down outside his Manhattan co-op. The former Beatle, 40, had just wrapped his first LP since the birth five years earlier of Sean, his son by **YOKO ONO;** one cut, "(Just Like) Starting Over," became an instant posthumous hit. Mark David Chapman, 25, who pleaded guilty to second-degree murder, was sentenced to 20 years to life at Attica State Prison in New York.

ALLAN TANNENBAUM

Suppose they made a $40 million movie and nobody came? That fate virtually befalls director Michael Cimino, 37, an Oscar-winner for 1978's *Deer Hunter,* whose three-hour-40-minute *Heaven's Gate* is pulled by the studio after one week at a single Manhattan uniplex and supplants *Cleopatra* as the industry's synonym for megaflop. Other moviemakers fare better: Martin Scorsese with *Raging Bull;* cult favorite David (*Eraserhead*) Lynch with the mainstream *The Elephant Man;* and the triumvirate of Jim Abrahams-David Zucker-Jerry Zucker with *Airplane!*

On the small screen, Richard Chamberlain reaffirms that he is Mr. Miniseries when America develops a powerful yen for *Shogun.* And skeptics snicker when Atlantan Ted Turner, at 41 a sportsman (he owns baseball's Braves and the NBA Hawks) and cable-TV entrepreneur, brashly launches the 24-hour, all-news CNN.

Cable News has no bureau in central Iran, which is just as well. Jimmy Carter, frustrated by the Ayatollah Khomeini's continuing refusal to free the Tehran embassy hostages, green-lights an Entebbe-style rescue raid. But 200 miles short of the target zone, in the aptly named Barren Desert, two of the team's eight helicopters collide with a refueling tanker; the ensuing conflagration kills eight American commandos and forces the mission to be aborted. Later in the year, Iran is invaded by neighboring Iraq, whose strongman, Saddam Hussein, hopes to quickly settle an old border dispute. U.S. policymakers express satisfaction and begin an unofficial "tilt" toward Saddam that would survive the eight-year Iran-Iraq war. Still, Pentagon war-gamers are more concerned with the traditional threat of a Warsaw Pact attack on Western Europe, which is why the Army's 8th Mechanized Infantry is stationed in Mainz, Germany, under the command of Brigadier General Norman Schwarzkopf, 46.

NASA scientists hoop it up when *Voyager I* beams home close-ups of Saturn's rings. The year's other big winner: Ronald Reagan, 69, who bests Jimmy Carter in presidential debates ("There you go again") and on Election Day.

Passages: Naturalist Joy (*Born Free*) Adamson, 69. TV's long-running *Fugitive,* David Janssen, 49. Teddy Roosevelt's daughter-turned-D.C.-social-lioness Alice Roosevelt Longworth, 96. Maker of overripe music (Annunzio Paolo) Mantovani, 74. Steve McQueen, 50. TV-ratings gamesman Arthur Nielsen, 83. Black Olympian Jesse Owens, 66 (whose four golds at the '36 Berlin Games infuriated white supremacist Adolf Hitler). Childhood-development authority Jean Piaget, 84. Author Katherine Anne (*Ship of Fools*) Porter, 90. Existentialist Jean-Paul Sartre, 74. Peter Sellers, 54. Thief Willie Sutton, 79 (who, when asked why he robbed banks, replied, "That's where the money is"). Mae West, 87.

Having been introduced by mutual friend Michael Caine, twice-divorced Mia Farrow, 35, and twice-divorced Woody Allen, 44, go on their first date. Actress Jodie (*Taxi Driver*) Foster, 18, in her sophomore year at Yale, receives a telephone call from obsessive fan John Hinckley Jr., 25, who would soon begin devising a tragic way to gain her attention. In Yugoslavia, Xarolj Seles presents his 6-year-old daughter Monica with her first tennis racket. And in New York City, Kit Culkin, 35, a struggling actor better known as Bonnie Bedelia's brother, and wife Pat, 26, welcome their first son, whom they name Macauley.

If vigorous enough to prune trees on his Santa Barbara spread, wasn't RONALD REAGAN, 69, fit to be President? The onetime actor and governor of California (normally right-handed) began his second bid to head the GOP ticket.

UPI / BETTMANN

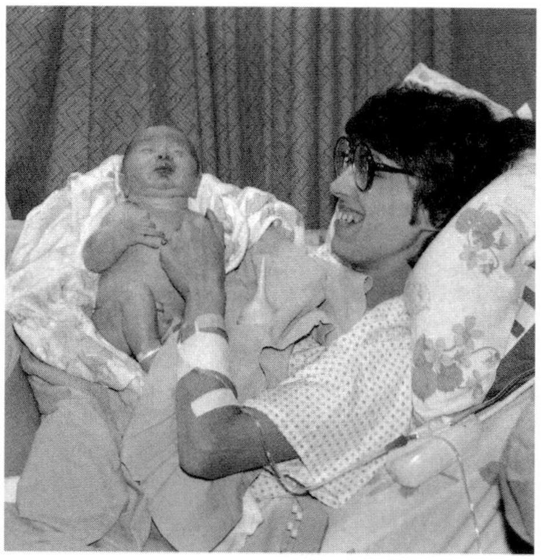

ELIZABETH KANE, 37, became a household pseudonym by bearing a son for an infertile couple whom she had never met, making the housewife from Pekin, Illinois, the country's first known surrogate mother.

SURROGATE PARENTING ASSOCIATES / VISIONS

MOUNT SAINT HELENS —one of but two active volcanoes in the Lower 48 —erupted seven times in five months; its ashes were borne by the jet stream as far east as Montana. Yet because the mountain rises in sparsely settled central Washington, the blasts killed only 57. Botanists visiting the ravaged 138,000-acre epicenter five years later were surprised to find seedlings pushing up through 100 feet of pumice.

ROGER WERTH / WOODFIN CAMP

Even if threads come back in style 15 years later, who could still squeeze into them? What's more, who'd want to? Which was why **BETSEY JOHNSON,** 38, who in the '60s had all but invented the mini, figured it high time to hike hems again. At least daughter **LULU,** 5, agreed.

HARRY BENSON

Having won the 1973 Pulitzer for the novel *The Optimist's Daughter* at the age of 64, **EUDORA WELTY** topped it at 71 by receiving the National Medal for Literature and by publishing the best-selling *Collected Stories.* Nor was the storyteller from Jackson, Mississippi, through; she would publish *One Writer's Beginnings* in 1984 and poetry into the 1990s.

TOM VICTOR

KENNY ROGERS dropped in to see what condition his condition was in. Pretty flush: His asthma was under control and his high-stakes career was no gamble. At 42, the onetime New Christy Minstrel and First Editioner worked with ex-Commodore Lionel Richie to record "Lady," a solo megahit that crossed over from country to climb not only the Hot 100 chart but also the soul and adult contemporary lists.

MARK SENNET

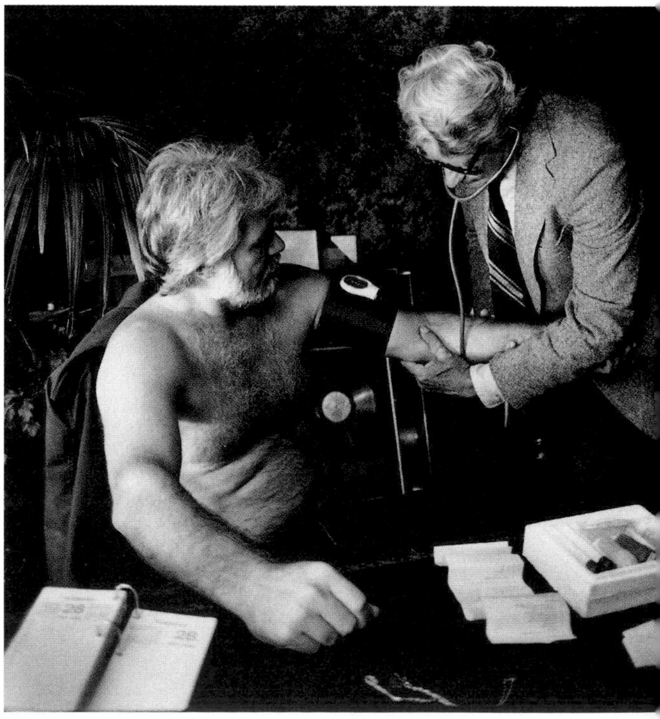

Morris wouldn't answer the call to din-din, so wild-and-crazy cat juggler **STEVE MARTIN,** 34, prepared to foil another kitty. If comedy isn't pretty, neither were Martin's happy feats: a list-topping gag book, *Cruel Shoes,* and his first movie, *The Jerk.* Word was he wanted his next to be directed by none other than Federico Feline-i.

HARRY BENSON

Back at Smith College in the '20s, **JULIA CHILD** was known as "Skinny." But after 17 years of French Chefdom on public television—and all those tempties to sample, from soup to nuts—the original kitchen aide, 68, was in the midst of paring 15 pounds off her 6'1" frame. Bon appetit, indeed.

LEE LOCKWOOD

Allegedly, even members of *Dallas'* cast knew not who shot J.R. At least star **LARRY HAGMAN,** 48, had an alibi: His character, aka "the human oil slick," stayed in a bullet-induced coma from the soap's cliff-hanging May finale until November, when the cows came home to South Fork. The epic Nielsens of that episode were untopped until the demobilization of *M*A*S*H* in 1983.

BARRY STAVER

Until Kiss, most folks probably thought heavy metal was something the Allies stopped Hitler's atom scientists from discovering. The band's gimmick, in addition to mega-amps, was that its members' faces were never seen sans greasepaint. Never. But for the record, the Fab(ergé) Four were (*from left*): rookie **ERIC CARR, ACE FREHLEY, PAUL STANLEY,** and the maximum factor, leader **GENE SIMMONS.**

RAEANNE RUBENSTEIN

A pensive **PAUL SIMON,** 39, might have been pondering: a) Why his pet project, the movie *One-Trick Pony,* flopped, while the soundtrack LP, his first in five years, was a smash. b) Whether to marry main squeeze Carrie Fisher, 24 (he did in 1983, but they separated after only 11 months). c) Why he and Art Garfunkle had split—because after all these years, it was still crazy.

RAEANNE RUBENSTEIN

Three months after the Soviet Army marched into Afghanistan, another Big Red Machine was stopped cold in upstate New York. At the Lake Placid Winter Games, the college stars of **TEAM USA** met the de facto pros from the U.S.S.R. in the semifinals —and, improbably, won, 4 to 3. America then out-skated Finland for the gold. (Because Moscow was host to the Summer Olympics, U.S. athletes, heeding President Carter's request, boycotted them.)

HEINZ KLUETMEIER / SPORTS ILLUSTRATED

On the verge of 24, **CAROLINE KENNEDY** was working as a film and TV researcher at New York City's Metropolitan Museum of Art and had just begun to see future husband Edwin Schlossberg. Her brother **JOHN,** about to turn 21, had two years remaining at Brown, where he was playing rugby (third string), acting in school plays and dating a senior.

STEPHEN J. SHERMAN / PICTURE GROUP

Was there nowhere on this sceptered isle a virginal maiden fit for a king-to-be? With Prince Charles nearing 32, his every social fancy was also that of Fleet Street's photographers, a lesson that was not lost on 19-year-old London nursery-school teacher **DIANA FRANCES SPENCER.** Long acquainted through their families, they courted for eight months before Charles proposed.

TIM GRAHAM / SYGMA

Hollywood's top directors were happy to take notes from **JOHN WILLIAMS,** who composed the scores for blockbusters like *The Towering Inferno, Jaws* and *Star Wars* (and was at work on a new Spielberg project about an archaeologist named for a state). But why **RAY CHARLES**? Because, at 42, Williams had also taken up the baton of the late Arthur Fiedler by signing to lead the Boston Pops and, unh-hunh, Charles was one of his early guest artists.

STEVE HANSEN

A most gentle man—except when writing about race relations in America—**JAMES BALDWIN,** 55, celebrated the release of his 19th book, *Just Above My Head,* in the south of France with companion **FREDERICK JAMES.** The essayist (*The Fire Next Time)* and novelist (*Go Tell It on the Mountain, Giovanni's Room)* published one more work of fiction before his death in 1987 of stomach cancer.

PIERRE BOULAT / COSMOS

Pioneering televangelist **JERRY** (*Old Time Gospel Hour*) **FALWELL,** 47, read the Election Day '80 returns and broke into a Patton-ted pose. By his reckoning, Moral Majority, the pro-life, pro-business, antiwelfare, antigay coalition he headed, had helped Ronald Reagan evict Jimmy Carter from the White House and also unseated several liberal warhorses from Congress.

CO RENTMEESTER

Talk about the light fantastic: He owned the Empire State Building (among many others) and she reigned over swank midtown hotels. But the **HELMSLEY'**s Manhattan melody soured in 1988 when the IRS filed tax evasion charges. **HARRY,** then 79, was declared incompetent to stand trial; **LEONA,** 67, was found guilty and served 18 months in a cell all of nine feet by seven.

CO RENTMEESTER

No, she was not a potted plant. But for peat's sake, was there anyone better at rooting out celebrity foibles than **LIZ SMITH,** 57? Her good-natured daily column in 60-plus newspapers provided the country with an iris on the showbiz and jet sets.

ROBIN PLATZER / TWIN IMAGES

1981

Twenty-five hundred guests actually attended "The Marriage of the Century," held July 29 at Westminster Abbey, but another 750 million witnesses around the planet tuned in live. Officiating at the union of **CHARLES PHILIP ARTHUR GEORGE**—at 32 the Prince of Wales and Earl of Chester, Duke of Cornwall, Duke of Rothesay, Earl of Carrick and Baron of Renfrew, Lord of the Isles and Great Steward of Scotland—and Lady **DIANA FRANCES SPENCER,** 20, the Archbishop of Canterbury prophetically proclaimed the event not "the place of arrival, but the place where the adventure really begins."

PATRICK LICHFIELD / CAMERA PRESS

World leaders may be cocooned in security, but they are still chillingly vulnerable. Eight weeks after his Inauguration as the 40th President of the United States, Ronald Reagan is leaving a Washington luncheon when John Hinckley Jr., 25, opens fire with a .22-caliber revolver; during the three-hour surgery that saves Reagan's life, Secretary of State Alexander Haig attempts to reassure the nation by going on live TV and proclaiming, "I'm in control here."

Some six weeks later, Pope John Paul II, 60, is meeting worshipers in St. Peter's Square at the Vatican when Turkish radical Mehmet Ali Agca, 23, opens fire with a 9-mm Browning; the pope is hospitalized five-plus weeks. (Agca would insist at his trial that the assault was funded by Bulgaria's secret service as a favor to Moscow, which was worried that John Paul II would crystallize anti-Soviet resentment in his native Poland.) In August, Omar Torrijos Herrera, 52, the Panamanian head of state who negotiated the reversion of rights to the Canal in 2000, dies when his plane mysteriously crashes; succeeding him: Manuel Antonio Noriega, 41. And in October, Anwar Sadat, 62, is reviewing a military parade when Muslim militants, infuriated by the Egyptian president's peace talks with Israel, open fire with submachine guns; Sadat is one of 10 slain.

The chain of succession is more peaceful on Broadcast News Row. Walter Cronkite had overcome the stigma of *The Morning Show*, a '50s program on which his cohost was a hand puppet, to win Gallup's designation as the most trustworthy American alive; now, at 65, he intones "That's the way it is" for the final time and cedes the CBS anchor's chair, his for 19 years, to Dan Rather, 49. And NBC anchor John Chancellor, 53, turns over the Teleprompter to Roger Mudd, 53, and Tom Brokaw, 41 (creating a vacancy on *The Today Show* that the network fills by issuing a loud alarm clock to sportscaster Bryant Gumbel, 33).

The year's top single: raspy-voiced Kim Carnes's *Bette Davis Eyes.* At 73, Bette Davis is most likely not eyeing a new 24-hour, youth-will-be-served cable channel that debuts by playing, appropriately enough, the Buggles's *Video Killed the Radio Star.* MTV's budget is low enough to make a bean-counter smile; record companies gladly pass along, gratis, videos made to play in dance clubs.

Passages: U.S. Army general Omar Bradley, 88 (leader of the D-Day invasion of Normandy). Historians Will Durant, 96, and wife Ariel Durant, 83. Silent-moviemaker Abel (*Napoleon*) Gance, 92. Rockster Bill ("Rock Around the Clock") Haley, 55. Hollywood costumer Edith Head, 80-plus. William Holden, 63. Brechtian singer Lotte ("Mack the Knife") Lenya, 83. Edwin Link, 77 (whose inventions included the flight simulator to train earthbound pilots). Boxer Joe Louis, 66. Aviator Juan Trippe, 81 (founder of Pan American Airways). *Readers' Digest* cofounder DeWitt Wallace, 91. Natalie Wood, 45.

Pulitzer shock: The first novel *A Confederacy of Dunces* wins the prize for fiction; its author, John Kennedy Toole, 32, had committed suicide 12 years earlier after his book was spurned by nine publishers. Broadway shock: A ticket to the Royal Shakespeare Company's 8½-hour *Nicholas Nickleby* costs $100. Sticker shock: In just 10 months, a first-class stamp shoots from 15¢ to 18¢ to 20¢.

So utterly did the under-$10 toy devised by Hungarian Erno Rubik, 37, sweep the world that it even made the august *Oxford English Dictionary*: "RUBIK('S) CUBE: a puzzle of a cube seemingly formed by 27 smaller cubes, uniform in size but of various colours, each layer of eight or nine smaller cubes being capable of rotation in its own plane; the task is to restore each face of the cube to a single colour after the uniformity has been destroyed by rotation of the various layers." Actually, it was a lot more fun than that.

RALPH MORSE

If his latest brainstorm didn't sell 100,000 units its first year, AKIO MORITA, 60, jokingly told the board of the firm he founded in 1946 on a $500 investment, he'd give up his chairmanship. The consumer-electronics impresario's job was safe. Despite an initial triple-digit price tag, in its first decade on the market Sony's Walkman pumped music into the ears of 30 million mobile owners.

MADDY MILLER

Just as well **RICHARD THOMAS**, 30, left Walton's Mountain two seasons earlier; there probably wasn't enough room up there for the twins his wife Alma, 34, was carrying. **BARBARA** and **GWENYTH** arrived as expected—and, before anyone could say John Boy-o-boy-o-boy, so did **PILAR.** The triplets were fine, but their parents separated in 1992.

MIMI COTTER

In a White Plains, New York, courthouse 10 miles from where she had fatally shot Scarsdale Diet doc Herman Tarnower, **JEAN HARRIS** stoically endured the press throughout a trial that lasted more than three months. The headmistress of a tony Virginia girls' school was convicted of second-degree murder. She served almost 12 years, during which time Harris worked for prison reforms and published two books, before being granted clemency in 1993.

ASSOCIATED PRESS

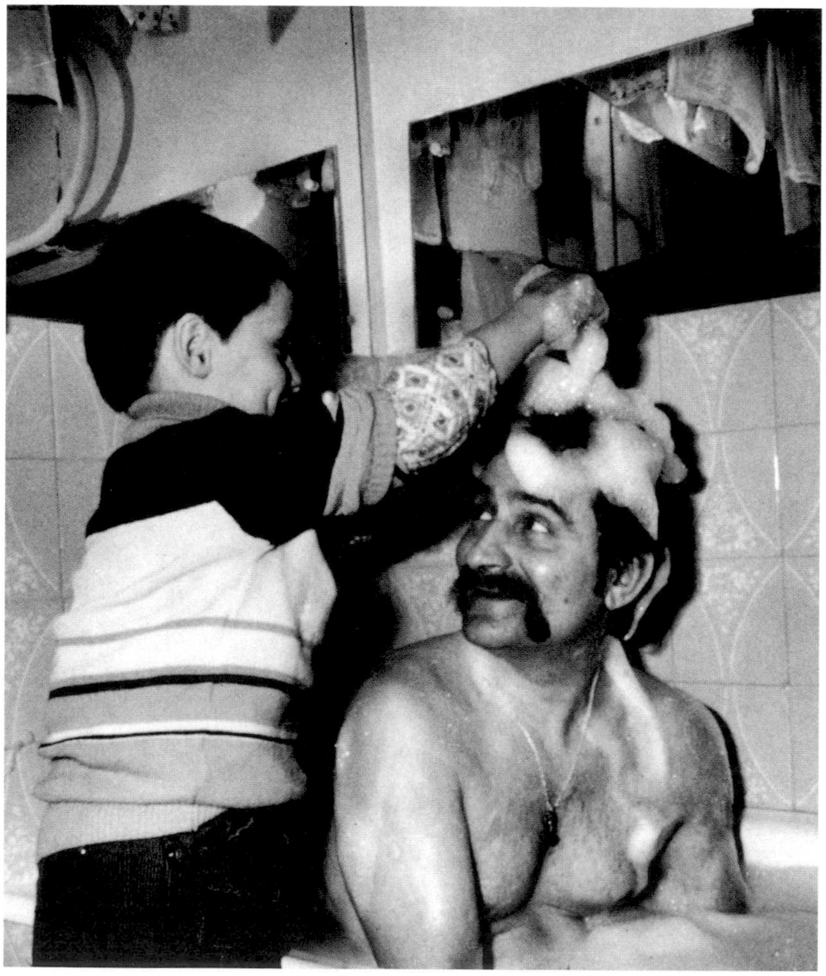

PRZEMAK WALESA, 6, shampooed the hair of dad **LECH,** who in the space of a year had gone from an unemployed electrician to the most famous man in Poland. For defying his country's Soviet overlords by organizing a union at the Gdansk shipyard, Walesa, 36, and the father of six, was already receiving anonymous hate mail. Worse was yet to come.

LASKI / SIPA

Mirror, mirror, on the wall, who's the shiest of them all? Or was the menu at La Grenouille of more fascination to **WOODY ALLEN** than dinner date **MIA FARROW**? The comedian-director, 45, and the actress, 36, were making the first of their dozen movies together, and in the second year of their 12-year affair.

DAVID MCGOUGH / DMI

Does the salad fork go on the left or the right? After acting in 22 movies, **ROBERT REDFORD,** 43, learned it wasn't easy from the other side of the camera either. But with a cast headed by **MARY TYLER MOORE,** Donald Sutherland, Timothy Hutton and Elizabeth McGovern, *Ordinary People* won the Oscar for Best Picture, Hutton for Best Supporting Actor and Redford for Best Director.

MARCIA REED

Clearly, no dirty dancing went on at the White House party celebrating **RONALD REAGAN**'s 70th birthday. The President, though, did seem to be trying to communicate something to **NANCY.** Maybe he sensed that her friendship with **FRANK SINATRA** might one day fuel gossip of extracurricular dooby-dooby-dooing at 1600 Pennsylvania Avenue.

MICHAEL EVANS / THE WHITE HOUSE

FRED ASTAIRE, 81, ended a quarter-century of widowerhood by taking as his bride pioneering jockey **ROBYN SMITH,** 38. Despite having ridden 250-plus winners, Smith hung up the horseshoes to please filmdom's softest shoe. Astaire died in 1987.

HARRY BENSON

The first 101 Justices of the Supreme Court were men. No. 102: **SANDRA DAY O'CONNOR,** 51, an Arizona-bred graduate of Stanford Law School (where she briefly dated Benchmate William Rehnquist). The first of three Reagan High Court appointees, O'Connor, who survived a bout of breast cancer in 1988, would confound many conservative backers with her nondoctrinaire votes.

DAVID HUME KENNERLY / GAMMA-LIAISON

On March 30, **RONALD REAGAN** became the fourth U.S. President to be hit by an assassin's bullet —and the first to survive. Doctors removed from his chest a slug that punctured a lung and narrowly missed his heart; he was back in the White House in two weeks. Gunman John Hinckley's other victims outside the Hilton Hotel in Washington: D.C. policeman Thomas Delehanty, 45, hit in the neck; Secret Serviceman Timothy McCarthy, 31, hit in the side; and White House press secretary **JIM BRADY,** 40, shot in the head. Despite losing some 20 percent of his frontal brain tissue in the surgery that saved his life, Brady (with son Scott, right) and his wife, Sarah, became ardent and effective advocates of gun control. Hinckley, 25, was institutionalized after being found not guilty by reason of insanity.

DICK SWANSON (RIGHT); RON EDMUNDS / ASSOCIATED PRESS

Say the secret word and win . . . a Central Park cruise with the **ALDAS. ALAN,** 45, who on his *M*A*S*H* hiatus directed his first movie, *The Four Seasons,* also made it a family affair by writing in small roles for daughters **ELIZABETH,** 20 (*on stern*), and **BEATRICE,** 19, while wife **ARLENE,** 48 (*left*), published a book of on-set photographs.

RAEANNE RUBENSTEIN

The **KINGS** of Bangor, Maine: (clockwise from left) **NAOMI;** parents **TABITHA,** 32, who had just published her first novel, *Small World,* and **STEPHEN,** at 33 the dean of macabre fast-reads; **JOE;** and **OWEN.** And it wasn't even Halloween. Guess who didn't have far to search for strange characters?

RAEANNE RUBENSTEIN

Short people, sang Randy Newman two years earlier, "got no reason to live." The 5'2" **PAUL WILLIAMS** didn't agree. At 40, he had composed hits like "We've Only Just Begun" and the Grammy-winning "Evergreen," and acted as a foil in movies like *Smokey and the Bandit* I & *II.* Other times, he just kicked back and waited for Newman to drive by.

MARK SENNET

Animal, mineral—or carrot-topped fitness guru **RICHARD SIMMONS**? At 33, the erstwhile fatty preached his diet gospel by way of a daily TV show and two books; his campy videos would arrive with the VCRing of America.

HARRY BENSON

SIMON BOND's crime was to publish *101 Uses for a Dead Cat* (as a tennis racket; as carpeting; as, four legs sticking straight up, a post for spooling yarn). Humane society officials were not amused. Nor, when the book of cartoons clawed its way to best-sellerdom, were Garfield and Heathcliff.

STEVF NORTHUP

He may have been a near high school flunk-out who was once reduced to selling shoes at a mall, but **EDDIE MURPHY,** 20, was no sucker. His comedic riffs and braying laugh had finally found a home (not to mention an audience) at *Saturday Night Live.* And his breakthrough movie, *48 HRS,* was only a year off; then it was on to Beverly Hills.

MIMI COTTER

1982

Grace Kelly of Philadelphia was on the Riviera, filming Hitchcock's *To Catch a Thief,* when she met her prince: Monaco's Rainier III, whom she wed in 1956. As **PRINCESS GRACE,** she bore him three heirs and co-ruled the postage-stamp principality for 26 years until, descending homeward down the steep hills above Monte Carlo, her British Rover swerved off the serpentine road. Daughter Stephanie, 17, survived; Grace died at 52.

HARRY BENSON

The Cold War can boast of few more surreal moments than the cordial meeting, at Leonid Brezhnev's funeral in Moscow, between first-term Vice President George Bush, 58, former head of the CIA, and new Soviet Premier Yuri Andropov, 68, former head of the KGB. Andropov, Kremlin spin doctors confide, has a love of many things American, including Jacqueline Susann potboilers and Chubby Checkers LPs. The spirit of detente, though, doesn't seem to reach Poland, where the hard-line regime jails shipyard union organizer Lech Walesa for 11 months. Nor the Pentagon, which to prepare for the next war is purchasing exotic hardware: $1,000 coffeepots for Air Force bombers and $400 hammers for Navy mechanics.

In Washington, a monument designed by 22-year-old Yale architecture student Maya Lin — twin 247-foot-long black granite walls listing Vietnam War dead — is dedicated. Sylvester Stallone pays his own tribute by unlacing his *Rocky* gloves long enough to play misunderstood Vietnam veteran John Rambo.

Not wishing the sun to set on the British Empire during her watch, Prime Minister Margaret Thatcher wages a bloody 74-day war against Argentina to reclaim the Falklands, a barren South Atlantic archipelago that's home to 1,900 British settlers and 700,000 sheep. Aside from the trauma suffered by Queen Elizabeth (she awakes in the wee hours to find London laborer Michael Fagan, who had circumvented Buckingham Palace security, at her bedside hankering for a chat), it is a banner year for the Sceptered Isle. Princess Diana and musical-theater titan Andrew Lloyd Webber both produce dynasty-extenders while the BBC's *Brideshead Revisited* triggers delirium amongst America's PBS crowd.

But just as *Real Men Don't Eat Quiche* — Bruce Fierstein's offbeat best-seller — the Nielsen families prefer *Dallas*. Not yet considered funny are an insufferable teen Reaganaut born to Woodstockian parents (despite Michael J. Fox, *Family Ties* is rated 34th out of 111 shows) nor wisecracking barflies (*Cheers* ranks 75th). Undeterred, NBC plants another seed that will one day flourish by creating a post-midnight show to follow Johnny Carson and installing as its host a morning talk-show personality named David Letterman.

Passages: Novelist John Cheever, 70. Ferdinand Waldo Demara, 60 (aka The Great Imposter). Moviemaker Rainer Werner Fassbender, 36. First *Today Show* host Dave Garroway, 69. Pianist Glenn Gould, 50. Hallmark cardsharp Joyce Hall, 91. Poet Archibald MacLeish, 89. Mystery novelist Ngaio Marsh, 82. Jazz pianist Thelonious Monk, 64. Ageless black baseball pitcher LeRoy "Satchel" Paige (whose aphorisms included: "Don't look back, something might be gaining on you"). Novelist Ayn Rand, 77. Country singer Marty ("El Paso") Robbins, 57. TV actor-producer Jack (*Dragnet*) Webb, 62.

Seven regional "Baby Bells" are spawned by AT&T's agreement to end its 83-year telephonic monopoly. New too is the compact disc, which will all but kill off the vinyl record by decade's end. Retired Utah dentist Barney Clark, 61, receives the first permanent artificial heart, extending his life by 112 days. And the disease most feared by the sexually active is genital herpes; known victims of a baffling new illness, acquired immune deficiency syndrome, total just 827.

Like, where did Moon Unit Zappa, 14, get the totally bitchen notion to cut an in-the-lingo single about San Fernando Valley mall-hoppers with names like On-dree-AH? Would you believe at a bar mitzvah? But, like, VALLEY GIRL was just a grody put-on—even in California, teens didn't really talk that way, right? Hey, like get a life?

MARK SENNET

Unveiled May 31, the VIETNAM VETERANS MEMORIAL in the nation's capital quickly proved a magnet for Americans whose lives had been unalterably touched by that conflict. Initially, the names of 57,939 war dead (among them, eight women) were incised in the black marble. Added later were the names of another 252 men confirmed to have been killed in action.

OWEN FRANKEN / SYGMA

JOHN R KUNKEL
RONALD S McCRARY
DENNIS J STANLEY
PHILLIP D WATTERS
RONALD P ZENGA
FRANK E BRAWNER
PAUL M EVANS
GARY D FALK
GARY L JAMIESON
RALPH E ICKE II
WILLIAM J ELSTEN
LEO A GEORGE
ERIC S GOLD
KENNETH A MASON
GREGORY H STANCIL
ROBERT R CHACON
JAMES J GROMPONE
CALVIN LEWIS
JOSE LIUS LOPEZ
TERRY LEE THOMPSON
PATRICK D BALLEW
JOHNNY R VERASTIQUE
DAVID E GAARDER
RONALD F NEAL
JEFFREY D ROPP
JIMMIE E TRENT
RAYMOND G BEAM
JACK R DANCE
ALAN D ELA
KENNETH W PETERS
JERRY LEE WARBRITTON
RICHARD A CARLSON
RONALD L HARRIS
DAVID L BELLERIVE
JAMES F BOYCE
EDWARD H MANN
JOHN M PAGE
ROBERT W SMITH
QUINCY H TRUETT
DIEGO AMADOR
DANIEL P GALLAGHER
RAYMOND J KREKELBERG

At his birth, by natural delivery, 7-pound, 12½-ounce **PRINCE WILLIAM ARTHUR PHILIP LOUIS** of Wales became second in line to the British throne, behind his heir-apparent father, **CHARLES.** Wills, as the baby was called, of course had his own nanny; but among the maternal duties **DIANA** retained was breast-feeding her first-born.

LORD SNOWDEN / CAMERA PRESS

America's first (and the world's 21st) test-tube baby, 5-pound, 12-ounce **ELIZABETH JORDAN CARR,** drove the religious right to warn of "delving into an area far too sacred for human beings to be involved in." But said dad **ROGER,** 30, who with wife **JUDY,** 28, had turned to in-vitro fertilization because of her damaged fallopian tubes, "we think other couples should have the joy we're experiencing."

TERRY ARTHUR

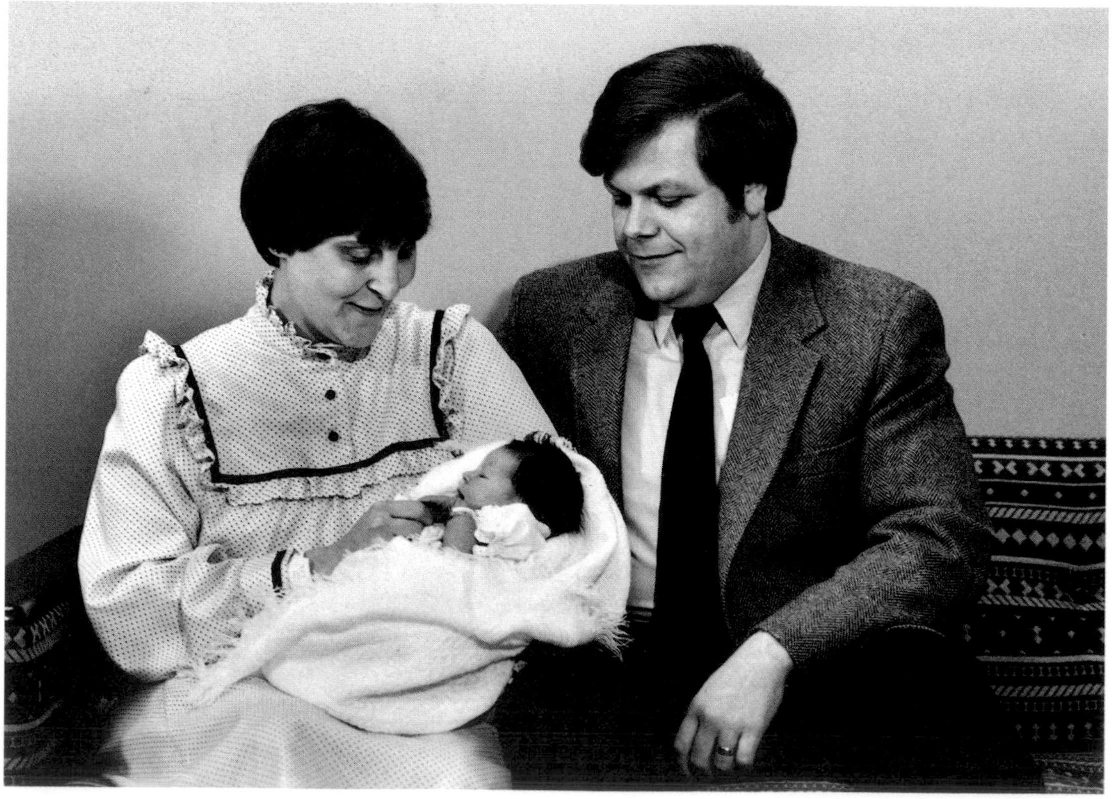

It was only a 40-inch-tall, $1.5 million latex-and-metal contraption that required 11 specialists to operate. Yet director Steven Spielberg's **E.T.** reached out and touched not only **HENRY THOMAS**, 9, and **DREW BARRYMORE,** 7, but also enough moviegoers to sell an otherworldly $310 million in tickets. That record stood until Spielberg broke it himself with 1993's *Jurassic Park.*

STEVE SCHAPIRO / GAMMA-LIAISON (NEAR RIGHT); TONY COSTA / OUTLINE

At age 35, **CHER** was supporting herself quite nicely working Vegas 20 weeks a year (at $30,000 a show, usually two shows a night). But when asked by director Robert Altman to join Sandy Dennis and Karen Black on Broadway in the drama *Come Back to the 5 & Dime, Jimmy Dean, Jimmy Dean* for $4,000 a week, she didn't sit on the offer for long.

MADDY MILLER

It's a dirty job, but **BOB CHRISMAN** had to do it. The National Park Service maintenance man, 33, and three colleagues spent five days each year in South Dakota cleansing the megabusts at Mount Rushmore of weeds, grass and pigeon guano. The Rockies may crumble, Gibralter may tumble—but never the Presidents Washington, Jefferson, Lincoln and T. Roosevelt.

STEVE NORTHUP

Killer bee. Samurai tailor. "Cheeseburger-cheeseburger, Pepsi-Pepsi." Food-fighting, toga-partying *Animal House*-mate. In six short years, **JOHN BELUSHI** created a zooful of zanies via four seasons of *Saturday Night Live* and seven movies. But he fueled his manic comedy with drugs, an overdose of which, injected by a female Canadian supplier, killed him in a Sunset Strip hotel. Belushi was 33.

MARCIA RESNICK

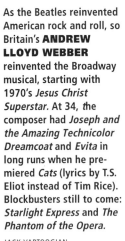

As the Beatles reinvented American rock and roll, so Britain's **ANDREW LLOYD WEBBER** reinvented the Broadway musical, starting with 1970's *Jesus Christ Superstar.* At 34, the composer had *Joseph and the Amazing Technicolor Dreamcoat* and *Evita* in long runs when he premiered *Cats* (lyrics by T.S. Eliot instead of Tim Rice). Blockbusters still to come: *Starlight Express* and *The Phantom of the Opera.*

JACK VARTOOGIAN

Two decades after his landmark *Catch-22*, **JOSEPH HELLER,** 59, contracted a neurological affliction that strikes only about 3,000 Americans a year. But physical therapy (here, with **DON SHAW**) enabled him to resume writing—including a book about his recovery from Guillain-Barré syndrome.

MICHAEL ABRAMSON

HENRY FONDA's health was already flagging when daughter **JANE** finally found the script that would allow them to act together onscreen for the first time: 1981's *On Golden Pond*. The third costar was **KATHARINE HEPBURN,** 72, whom Henry had never met despite their collective 98 years in Hollywood. *Pond* earned Kate her fourth Oscar and Henry his first, just four months before his death at 77.

MARY ELLEN MARK

First rule of vaudeville: For a cheap laugh, drop your trousers. Rule No. 2: For a still cheaper laugh, cross-dress. **DUSTIN HOFFMAN,** 45, heeded Rule No. 2—and layered on some delicate emoting—to make the gender-bending *Tootsie* the year's top comedy. Ironically, he would lose the Oscar to an actor wearing a diaper-like *dhoti* (Ben Kingsley, who portrayed *Gandhi).*

RAEANNE RUBENSTEIN

First, the good news for **TOM SELLECK:** In its second full season, his *Magnum, P.I.*—a series CBS launched in part to reuse the expensive facilities left over from its long-run *Hawaii Five-O*—tied *M*A*S*H* for No. 3 in the Nielsens. Now the bad news: Because of the show's success, Selleck, at 37 eager for big-screen stardom as well, had to pass on creating the role of Indiana Jones.

KEN REGAN / CAMERA 5

Parents who thought Junior's lunch money was going to the schoolyard bully just didn't get it. The real culprit: **PAC-MAN,** video arcadia's Smile-Button-in-Profile, who gobbled up onscreen ghosts and play-me-again quarters with equal zest. But Packy was soon to be out-joysticked by more graphically refined games such as Donkey Kong and Frogger.

ATARI

Product of a broken home, an unwed mother at 17, briefly a prostitute to support her infant son, **MAYA ANGELOU,** 53, retreated to academia after the collapse of her second marriage. Yet 11 years later, she would stand and deliver a mesmeric poem at Bill Clinton's swearing-in, the first inaugural verse since Robert Frost's the day Jack Kennedy took office.

MARY ELLEN MARK

Master of all he surveyed—Morrisonville, Virginia (pop: 16) and assorted family members—was Pulitzer Prize-winning humorist **RUSSELL BAKER,** renovating an 1810 cabin in his hometown. Another reason to be high: *Growing Up,* his memoirs of a rustic youth, was a best-seller. But Baker, 57, was no rube; in 1993, the *New York Times* columnist was tapped by *Masterpiece Theater* to fill the leather club chair vacated by Alistair Cooke.

TOM VICTOR

How was their Broadway revival of Noel Coward's *Private Lives* faring? Critics praised **RICHARD BURTON** more than **ELIZABETH TAYLOR.** Backstage with the twice-divorced-from-each-other stars: Mexican lawyer **VICTOR LUNA,** 56, whose engagement ring Taylor, 51, would soon return, and **SALLY HAY,** 35, the fourth wife of Burton, 58, whom he would soon widow.

DAVID McGOUGH / DMI

In the Western Hemisphere, which national capital is situated the farthest west? Stumpers like this make Trivial Pursuit, created by Canadians Chris Haney, 33, and Scott Abbott, 34, the hottest board game since Monopoly. Query 2: Who becomes the first human known to have walked from the lowest tip of South America to the topmost tip of North America? Query 3: Who becomes the first American woman (and third overall) to achieve earth orbit? Query 4: Who wins the 1983 Nobel Prize for Peace? Query 5: Who scrawled 60 volumes of diaries for which the German newsmagazine *Stern* pays $3.2 million in the belief that the author was Adolf Hitler? Query 6: Who is at long last authenticated as the composer of a 1765 chamber symphony that had been unearthed in 1943 in a musical library in Odense, Denmark? (Answers below.)

All ends well in the hit movie *WarGames,* but when the two superpowers are put to military tests (though not against each other), they win less than high marks. The Soviet defense system needs two hours to lock onto and destroy a plane wandering through its airspace; all 269 aboard civilian Korean Air Lines Flight 007 are killed. In Beirut, the bombing by Shiites of the U.S. Embassy spurs Ronald Reagan to send in the Marines, 242 of whom die sleeping when a truck packed with explosives is rammed into their barracks at dawn. Just six days later, the President orders troops to the Caribbean republic of Grenada (pop: 108,000) to oust a new leftist junta and to protect 1,000 Americans (residents of the island plus students attending an offshore medical school); the mission is executed so handily by 7,000 combatants that the Pentagon passes out 8,612 medals. Less embarrassing is the demobilization of *M*A*S*H.* The 251st and final episode of the CBS sitcom (which has run longer than the Korean War that is its setting) pulls not only heartstrings but also the highest Nielsens ever.

Passages: Filipino opposition politician Benigno Aquino, 61 (invited home from exile by President Ferdinand Marcos, he is shot dead by government troops moments after landing at Manila Airport). Moviemaker Luis Bunuel, 83. Popster Karen ("Close to You") Carpenter, 32. Buster (*Tarzan, Flash Gordon*) Crabbe, 75. Boxer Jack Dempsey, 87. Architect R. Buckminster Fuller, 88. TV host Arthur Godfrey, 79. Gangster Meyer Lansky, 80. Painter Joan Miro, 90. Historical novelist Mary Renault, 78. Gloria Swanson, 84. Earl Tupper, 76 (who in 1942 began making plastic tableware to be sold at neighborhood parties). Bluesman Muddy Waters, 68. Playwright Tennessee (*A Streetcar Named Desire*) Williams, 71.

In Search of Excellence, a survey of well-managed companies by Tom Peters and Robert Waterman, ironically becomes a best-seller even as 12 million are jobless, the highest U.S. unemployment rate since Depression's end. On Wall Street, a Drexel Burnham Lambert securities specialist has a brainstorm for reviving the economy; citing historical data showing that high-yield bonds in high-risk firms invariably appreciate, Michael Milken, 37, persuades insititutional investors to begin purchasing what skeptics continue to call "junk bonds."

Answers: 1) Mexico City. 2) George Meegan, 30, of Rainham, England, who hikes the 19,021 miles from Tierra del Fuego to the Beaufort Sea in 2,426 days. 3) Sally Ride, 32. 4) Polish union leader Lech Walesa, 39. 5) Military relics dealer Konrad Kajau, 45, of Stuttgart. 6) Wolfgang Amadeus Mozart, at age 9.

She was CYDNEY CHASE and you weren't. The summer's No. 1 comedy, *National Lampoon's Vacation,* starred her dad and not yours. Finally, her family's 39-year-old CHEVY played the piano and yours couldn't.

STEVE SCHAPIRO / GAMMA-LIAISON

In the backbyting world of computer software, BILL GATES, 28, had it pretty cushy. Sales of MS-DOS, the operating system he helped develop to run IBM's PC, surged after Big Blue (unlike rival Apple) allowed its machine to be legally cloned by other companies. When Microsoft, the firm he cofounded, went public in 1986, Gates became an instant $390-millionaire, a fortune that would later surpass $7 billion.

DALE WITTNER

1983

MICROSOFT

Give My Regards to Broad Street, his first movie since 1965's *Help!,* was a dud. Not to worry. In harmony with the Beatles, Wings and others, **PAUL McCARTNEY**, 41, had sold the most LPs ever (100 million). And with the help of wife **LINDA**'s lawyer father, he ran a firm that owned the copyrights to musical properties as varied as *Annie,* the late Buddy Holly's catalog and even "Sentimental Journey."

DAVE HOGAN / LGI

That was **ALISON EASTWOOD**, 10, making her dad's day. **CLINT** had separated from his wife, Maggie, to live with actress Sondra Locke. But at 52, he was using his directorial clout to put in quality screen time with his kids: Son Kyle, 14, costarred in his C&W road picture, *Honkytonk Man,* and Alison would have a key role in the following year's *Tightrope.*

KEN REGAN / CAMERA 5

Her rows of Oscars, Emmys and Grammys notwithstanding, it took **BARBRA STREISAND,** 41, a decade and a half to get a pet project (other than poodle Sadie) off the ground. But with *Yentl's* release, she became the first ever to receive four credits (cowriter, producer, director, star) on a single Hollywood musical. (PS: All nine soundtrack cuts were hers too).

DOUGLAS KIRKLAND / SYGMA

He had heeded supply-side economic advisers and muscled through an epic tax cut. He had heeded hard-line foreign policy advisers and okayed covert aid to Nicaragua's *contras* even if it meant defying Congress. And he had heeded Yoda-like science advisers and proposed a $5.2 billion real-life *Star Wars* to shield the American mainland from missiles launched by "The Evil Empire." Surely **RONALD REAGAN,** 72, was due a little rest?

MICHAEL EVANS / SYGMA

He overcame dyslexia; he contemplated joining the priesthood; he made an inauspicious movie debut in the Brooke Shields stinker *Endless Love.* But on the strength of a scene that he talked the director into letting him improvise —the lip-synching, air-guitaring romp in *Risky Business*—**TOM CRUISE** suddenly found himself, at 21, a Hollywood player.

NEAL PRESTON

She overcame hypochondria (and an all-too-real car mishap that left her briefly paralyzed on one side and blind in one eye); she lived for a time on a kibbutz; she was Wonder Woman's kid sis on TV. But her subtle seriocomic turn in *Terms of Endearment,* coming on top of *Urban Cowboy* and *An Officer and a Gentleman,* made **DEBRA WINGER,** 28, the toast of L.A. (as well as of Lincoln, Nebraska, where she often flew to see Governor Bob Kerrey).

PAUL JASMIN / VISAGES

Incredibly, the American studio with U.S. rights to 1982's *Road Warrior* thought it a throwaway road flick; by the time critics began praising the hyperkinetic doomsday saga from Australia, it was opening at drive-ins across the Southwest. But its star, Sydney-raised (and New York State-born) **MEL GIBSON,** 27, had already wrapped the picture that would let him say g'day to mainstream audiences: *The Year of Living Dangerously*.

KEN REGAN / CAMERA 5

Rock's Lady Di had in mind a different kind of thunderous ovation at her freebie concert in New York City's Central Park. **DIANA ROSS,** 39, mounted the show to kick off a new album and a 34-city tour. But the heavens wept, sending 350,000 squishing homeward. Next night, Ross drew another SRO crowd, but postconcert violence led to new rules that in effect halted megarock gigs in the Park until 1991.

DOUG REUTHER

GLORIA STEINEM's was the friendly face of feminism. Though *Ms.,* which she had cofounded in 1972 and still edited, could burn with radical lib anger, Steinem's own no-less-passionate writings were witty and accessible; in fact, her first book of essays, *Outrageous Acts and Everyday Rebellions,* became a best-seller as its author tacked gracefully toward her 50th birthday.

MARIANNE BARCELLONA

It was a match waiting to be made: the song-and-dance genius of **MICHAEL JACKSON,** 25, with the growing reach of MTV. The two-year-old cable network inserted into heavy rotation four elaborately produced videos from the Gloved One's second solo LP; boosted by the free air time, *Thriller* spun off seven Top 10 singles and, with sales of 40 million-plus, became the No. 1 album of all time.

DOUGLAS KIRKLAND / SYGMA

Michael's moon-walk may have seemed fresh to MTVideots uptown and in the hinterlands, but it was just a warm-up drill for inner-city breakers like **LORENZO SOTO** (*front*) and **KEN GABBERT,** both 16. The decade-old street-dance form went Hollywood with mixed success. In *Flashdance,* a male breaker in drag doubled Jennifer Beals's dazzling finale, but low-budget quickies like *Breakdance* and *Electric Boogaloo* hip-hopped into cineplex oblivion.

JACK VARTOOGIAN

BEWARE
OF DOG
KEEP
OUT

The Great **CABBAGE PATCH DOLL** Shortage was a triumph of ugly-duckling merchandising over Barbie-and-Ken glitz. These weren't dolls up for sale but foundlings in search of a new mommy (whose folks had the requisite $17.99). And each was said to be one-of-a-kind, right down to the name on the adoption papers. With monikers like Olive Jodi and Ferieca Netty, they probably were.

EVELYN FLORET

Like a certain watch, **WENDY O. WILLIAMS** could take a licking and keep on ticking. Onstage, the lead singer of the heavy metal Plasmatics, 32, flashed her breasts, talked dirty and feigned sex acts that guaranteed arrest (and, in Milwaukee, a beating by cops after she slapped one who had pawed her while making the bust). Offstage, her problem was finding an industrial-strength pillow.

MARY ELLEN MARK

Another Boxer Rebellion? A new Brief Encounter? **MENS UNDERWEAR** crossed the gender line after Jockey and Calvin Klein resized tops and redesigned bottoms (fly fronts, after all, being now quite superfluous).

DOUGLAS KIRKLAND / SYGMA

This **OSCAR** (*inset, left*) was also a grouch, which suited Fletcher Haynes of Lambert, Mississippi, just fine. When Dobermans couldn't safeguard his 25-acre auto junkyard, he remembered a seven-foot, 300-pound bird that he had observed angrily pecking attendees at an animal auction. Problem solved, reported Haynes. Seems thieves had a fear of being ostrich-cized.

SLICK LAWSON

1984

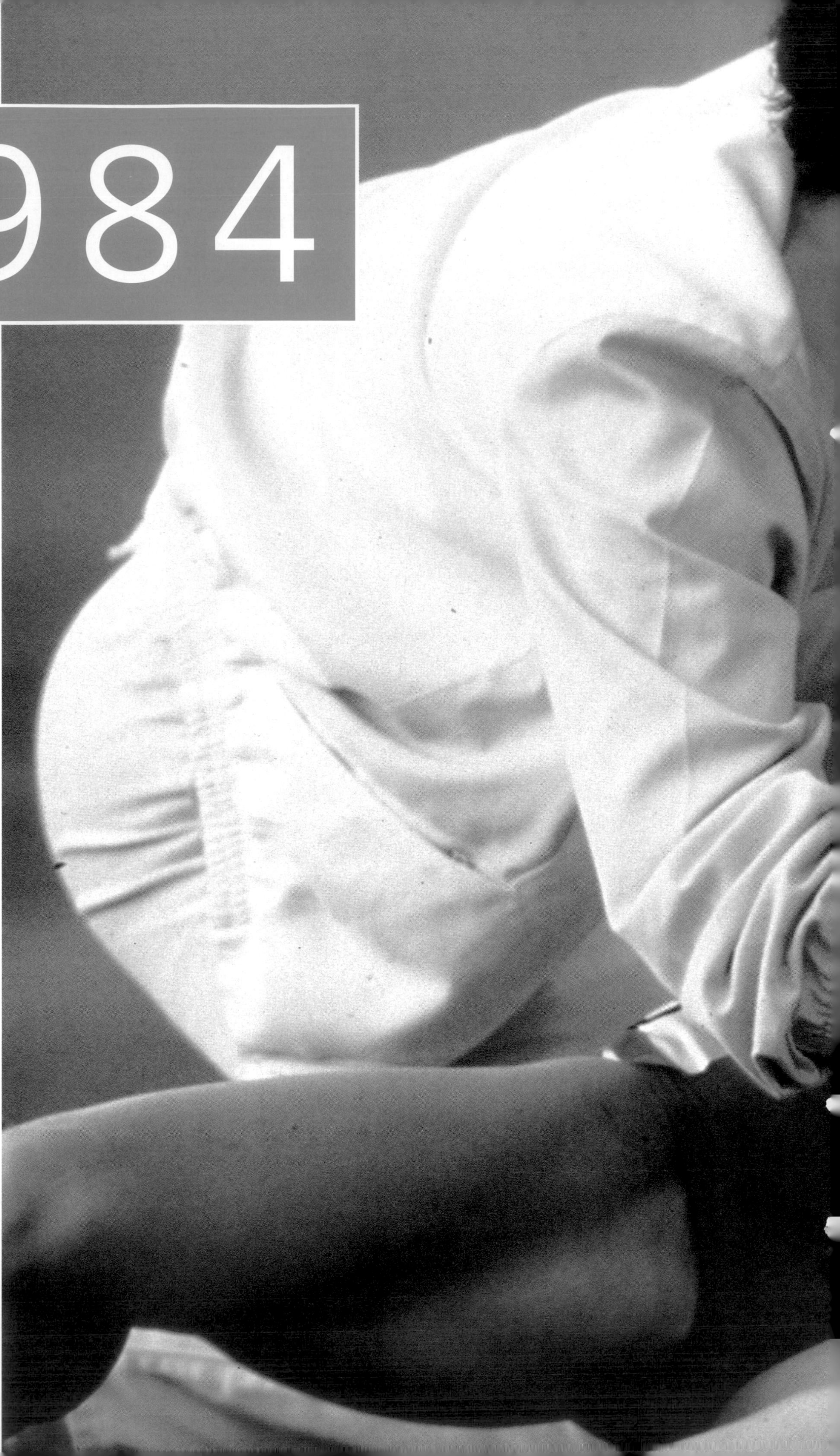

Her training for the '80 Olympics wasted because of the U.S. boycott of the Moscow Games, **MARY DECKER** hoped at 26 to win 3000-meter gold at Los Angeles. Her chief rival: shoeless South African wunderkind Zola Budd, 18. But on Lap 4, the two accidentally bumped—leaving Decker sprawled in anguish on the track and Budd so distraught that she came in a distant seventh.

DAVID BURNETT / CONTACT

No style points for this bellyflop, but then **MARY LOU RETTON,** 16, was a gymnast, not a diver. In addition to capturing two bronzes and a silver, she became the Bo Derek of the Summer Games by nailing a 10 to clinch the All Around gold. Her next vault: onto America's breakfast tables, as the first Wheaties cover girl.

BEN WEAVER

Entering the L.A. Games, **EDWIN MOSES,** 29, had not lost a 400-meter hurdles race in seven years. Leaving them, he still hadn't; employing a flawless 13-strides-and-jump technique, he picked up another gold medal to go with the one earned at Montreal in 1976. Moses would keep his stunning streak alive until 1987 when, after 122 straight firsts, he finally had to settle for a second.

NEAL PRESTON

The Russians aren't coming, the Russians aren't coming . . . to the Los Angeles Olympiad, that is. Seven months after the world discovered the splendors of Sarajevo when that postcard-pretty Yugoslavian city played host to the XIV Winter Games, 140 nations send teams to the XXIII Summer Games. Conspicuously absent: Soviet athletes. The Kremlin's payback for the American boycott of Moscow four years earlier matters little to gold medalists like sprinter Evelyn Ashford, diver Greg Louganis and quintuple-winner Carl Lewis, but it proves good news for homegrown gymnasts, who are not a traditional force in international competition. Capitalism also triumphs when the Games turn out to be the first ever to show a profit, thanks to the 46-year-old travel-agency mogul who orchestrated the 15-day extravaganza, Peter Ueberroth.

In addition to joy, California produces grief. In San Ysidoro, 21 patrons of a McDonald's are killed, and 19 wounded, when security guard James Huberty, 41, sprays the restaurant with 257 rounds before shooting himself. And in Manhattan Beach, the Virginia McMartin Preschool is padlocked after its owner, 76, and six employees are arrested on 115 counts of molesting their young pupils; over the next six years all defendants would be acquitted of all charges, but the incident cracks wide the Pandora's box of child abuse.

Just two years after the release of the Oscar-winning *Gandhi,* India's Prime Minister, 66-year-old Indira Gandhi (who is no relation to the assassinated pacifist) is on her way to tape a television interview with British entertainer Peter Ustinov when she is shot dead by two of her Sikh bodyguards. In the central Indian city of Bhopal, an accident at a chemical plant owned by Union Carbide vents a cloud of deadly methyl isocyanate gas; the toll: an estimated 1,700.

Passages: Photographer Ansel Adams, 82. Baby Fae, 33 days (21 of them on a heart transplanted from a baboon). Pollster George Gallup, 82. Marvin ("I Heard It Through the Grapevine") Gaye, 44 (shot dead by his dad). The Reverend Martin Luther King Sr., 84. Publisher Alfred Knopf, 91. Ray Kroc, 81 (who in 1955 began franchising McDonald's outlets). Ethel Merman, 75. Moviemaker Sam (*The Wild Bunch*) Peckinpah, 59. Off-hours TV pitchman Sam (Chop-O-Matic; the Pocket Fisherman) Popeil, 69. John Rock, 94, principal developer of the birth-control pill. Moviemaker François Truffaut, 52. Fred Waring, 84 (the musicmaker who in 1936 invented a food processor he dubbed the blender).

"Where's the beef?" squawks Chicago grandmother Clara Peller, 83, in a TV commercial that wins fast-food converts to Wendy's. Democrat Walter Mondale borrows the line to deftly skewer rival Gary Hart and capture his party's nomination, but becomes mincemeat himself in the Reagan re-election landslide.

No major publishing house will buy a Maryland insurance agent's novel about a Soviet submariner who wants to deliver himself and his high-tech boat to the U.S., so Tom Clancy, 37, persuades the Naval Institute Press to accept its first fiction ever, *The Hunt for Red October.* And with *Neuromancer,* a dark sci-fi yarn set in *Bladerunner* territory, William Gibson, 45, coins a neologism for the growing ganglia of global computer networks: "cyberspace," an electronic void where Max Headroom will soon dwell and the planned data superhighway run.

With her victory in the French Open, MARTINA NAVRATILOVA, 27, became tennis's third woman Grand Slammer (the other tournaments: Wimbledon and the U.S. and Australian Opens). Despite a highly public personal life that would include a lesbian palimony suit, the Czech-born Navratilova reigned until Steffi Graf came of age in the late '80s.

© CAROL L. NEWSOM

Preppies became old shoe with the spawning of the Young Urban Professional, aka **YUPPIE.** But the fast-tracking, power-dressing, Rolex-watching, Filofax-toting, Jamaica Blue Mountain coffee-drinking, sushi- & goat cheese- & homemade pasta-noshing, fitness-fanaticking crowd would say *no mas* in the '90s, when the gals took to Running with the Wolves and the guys discovered the joys of Iron Johnning.

RAEANNE RUBENSTEIN

In her continuing musical evolution, **LINDA RONSTADT** harked back to the big-band era and was rewarded with a hit album of old chestnuts, *What's New.* And at 38, her heart had wheeled around to movie mogul George Lucas, 39, single again after separating from his film editor wife, Marcia (who was seeing a stained-glass craftsman).

PETER C. BORSARI

Monaco's **PRINCESS CAROLINE,** 27, proudly displayed her first child, son **ANDREA.** The father: her second husband, Italian playboy and speedboat racer Stefano Casiraghi, 23, whom she had wed 5½ months earlier while continuing to seek an annulment of her first marriage to French playboy Philip Junot.

LORENT SOLA / GAMMA-LIAISON

With Ronald Reagan riding high post-Grenada, Democratic nominee Walter Mondale sought to win brownie points (and the votes of former Brownies) by adding New York congresswoman **GERALDINE FERRARO,** 49, to the ticket. It didn't help. The Electoral College tally: Reagan-Bush 525, Mondale-Ferraro 13. Plus, questions raised about her husband's real estate practices were to plague Ferraro's unsuccessful 1992 run for the Senate.

STANLEY TRETICK

As American as you-know-what were the droll takes on housewifery dispensed by **ERMA BOMBECK,** 57, by way of a column that ran in 900-plus papers, and books like *Motherhood, The Second Oldest Profession.* Nor, after 21 years at it, was the material running thin; 1993's *A Marriage Made in Heaven . . . Or Too Tired for an Affair* would be her eighth best-seller.

RAEANNE RUBENSTEIN

Having sifted the sands of Egypt for 10 years to produce *Ancient Evenings,* his 709-page 1983 book-shelf-buster, **NORMAN MAILER,** 61, needed just 60 days to bat out a high-testosterone mystery, *Tough Guys Don't Dance.* With five ex-wives and eight children, Mailer dared not let the word processor cool; he was already at work on his 1991 opus, *Harlot's Ghost.*

RICHARD HOWARD

FRAGILE
1094

The christening of **ELIZABETH JAGGER,** 4 months, was attended by (from right) maternal grandmother **MARJORIE HALL**; mom **JERRY HALL,** 28; dad **MICK,** 40; and paternal grandparents **EVA** and **JOE JAGGER.** When Jerry and Mick married six years and two more babies later, Elizabeth would serve as a flower girl.

GLOBE

Even in death, **JOHN WAYNE** was bigger than life. Five years after the actor's death of cancer, at 72, sculptor **HARRY JACKSON** (*lead horseman, left*) cast a 21-foot-high, six-ton bronze of a mounted Wayne. Trail's end for the $2 milllion statue: Beverly Hills, where it now watches over a Wilshire Boulevard bank the Duke repped.

MARK SENNET

Okay, so the reviews for his *Harry and Son* were less than kind; **PAUL NEWMAN,** 59, and **JOANNE WOODWARD,** 54, still had each other (not to mention four of the bluest eyes on the planet). He would direct her again in 1987's *The Glass Menagerie,* and they would costar for the tenth time in 1990's *Mr. and Mrs. Bridge.*

STEVE SCHAPIRO / GAMMA-LIAISON

Having broken the network color barrier by costarring in 1965's *I Spy,* **BILL COSBY** returned to prime time to rewrite another history: Nielsen's. *The Cosby Show* ended its first season No. 3, then topped the ratings for the next five seasons, tying the record set by *All in the Family.* And unlike Carroll O'Connor, Cosby, 47, also dominated the airwaves on other nights with his pitches for Coke, Jell-O Pudding, Ford and Texas Instruments.

NBC

Named the year's No. 1 male box-office draw thanks to *Ghostbusters,* **BILL MURRAY,** 34, decided to stop sliming around. But the *Saturday Night Live* alum still drew giggles when he played it straight in *The Razor's Edge*, the Maugham tale of a World War I vet searching for the meaning of life. So it was back to comedy: *Scrooged, Ghostbusters II, Quick Change, What About Bob, Groundhog Day* . . .

BARBARA WALZ / OUTLINE

Who'd have thought that a mermaid-out-of-water comedy would free director **RON HOWARD,** 30, and male lead **TOM HANKS,** 28, from sitcom hell (Howard: *Happy Days;* Hanks: *Bosom Buddies)* and ingenue **DARYL HANNAH,** 24, from a career in slice-and-dicers (*The Final Terror)*? Only Hannah would fail to fully cash in, post-*Splash;* by 1993, after several big-budget yawners, she was playing the title role in a cable remake of *Attack of the 50 Ft. Woman.*

MARK SENNET

Claus (*center)* and Beatrix thought owner Glenn Milstead, 38, **DIVINE.** As did devotees of the drag clubs that the wispy-voiced 320-pounder played when he wasn't making big-screen, poor-taste classics like *Pink Flamingos, Polyester* and *Lust in the Dust.* Divine would grace a mainstream hit (*Hairspray)* and even appear in men's clothing (*Trouble in Mind)* before his death, at 42, in 1988.

MARK SENNET

She's So Unusual was the title of **CYNDI LAUPER**'s debut album, and the 31-year-old belter whose thick outer-borough accent drove "Girls Just Wanna Have Fun" tried to live up to it. But after winning the Best New Artist Grammy, Lauper decided to unditz her act for her second LP, *True Colors.* That was like a mistake, ya know?

RAEANNE RUBENSTEIN

YUL BRYNNER's hello to newly crowned Miss America **VANESSA WILLIAMS** was, for **EDDIE MURPHY,** a real king-and-eyeful. Williams, 20, would lose her crown after *Penthouse* ran some raunchy pre-pageant nudes of her, but would later establish herself as a Grammy-nominated singer with an aptly titled chart-topping single: "Save the Best for Last."

ROBIN PLATZER / TWIN IMAGES

Minneapolis was home to stolid institutions like Pillsbury, 3M and the NFL Vikings—and now His Royal Badness, native son **PRINCE** (rest of name: Roger Nelson), a small (5'2"), risquély packaged musical hitmaker ("Little Red Corvette"). At 26, Prince also directed his first movie, *Purple Rain,* that briefly outgrossed *Ghostbusters* and threw off a soundtrack LP that was the year's top seller.

JANE HALE / THE FLINT JOURNAL

The only Beach Boy who could actually hang 10, **DENNIS WILSON** lived a life as dangerous as the Pipeline in winter. Split from Wife No. 5 (a first cousin, 19, whom he wed after she bore his fourth child) and in rehab for coke and booze, he began diving one day for some items tossed away years earlier from a Marina del Rey pier. Nostalgia proved fatal; Wilson was 39.

DEAN O. TORRENCE

BBC-TV footage of the famine in East Africa had impelled Boomtown Rat **BOB GELDOF,** 33 (in Ethiopia, *right*), to gather fellow UK rockers to cut the 1984 Band Aid single, "Do They Know It's Christmas?" His encore: Producing a bi-Continental benefit concert that even featured Elvis (Costello, that is). The 16-hour, globally telecast Live Aid opened in London and closed in Philadelphia (where the acts included, clockwise from *top left):* **KEITH RICHARDS, DARYL HALL, JOHN OATES, RON WOOD, BOB DYLAN, MADONNA, MICK JAGGER** and **TINA TURNER.** Phil Collins sprang for a Concorde ticket and raced the time zones to grace both venues, which jointly raised $88 million.

KEN REGAN / CAMERA 5 (LEFT); IAN COOK

1985

Gerontocracy, or rule by the aged, passes from the Soviet Union with Konstantin Chernenko, 73, whose health was already failing when he was appointed General Secretary the previous year. After burying in 30 months three leaders whose average age was 72-plus, the Kremlin elevates Mikhail Gorbachev, at 54 the youngest to take office since Josef Stalin in 1922. In Geneva six months later, Ronald Reagan, 74, sizes up his new counterpart and tries to disarm him with a favorite anecdote (about the boy who, presented with a ton of manure, begins shoveling because "There must be a pony in here!").

America's farmers are also in deep doo-doo, with foreclosures running at a record rate. Their plight is acknowledged by Willie Nelson, who organizes the first Farm Aid concert, and by Hollywood, whose spate of 4-H melodramas yields a bumper crop of Oscar nominations for pluckiest agriculturette (Sally Field, *Places in the Heart;* Jessica Lange, *Country;* Sissy Spacek, *The River*). Eighteen years after agreeing to hype *The Flying Nun* at the Golden Globe Awards by swooping down from the rafters into the arms of a bemused John Wayne, Field, who at 37 has reclaimed her career with *Sybil* and *Norma Rae,* accepts her second Best Actress Award. "I can't deny the fact you like me," she gushes, "right now, you like me!" Yes, but they respect her even more.

A humpbacked whale nicknamed Humphrey swims 70 miles up California's Sacramento River before cetophiles can turn him around. Also heading the wrong way is *CBS Morning News,* which hopes to catch ABC's *Good Morning America* and NBC's *The Today Show* by hiring Phyllis George, 35; Miss America 1971's early-morning reign lasts but eight months. The unknown star of a new syndicated talk show will enjoy a significantly longer run: Oprah Winfrey, 31.

After 113 years, Montgomery Ward cancels its mail-order catalog. But there's no need to drive out to the mall; the cable Home Shopping Network opens up nationally (the first item offered is — what else? — a gold chain).

Passages: Designer Laura Ashley, 60. Artist Marc Chagall, 97. James Dewar, 88 (inventor in 1930 of the Hostess Twinkie). Primatologist Dian Fossey, 53 (murdered while studying gorillas in the mists of Rwanda's highlands). Designer Rudi Gernreich, 62 (the 1964 perpetrator of women's topless swimsuits). Cartoonist Chester (Dick Tracy) Gould, 84. Margaret Hamilton, 82 (*Oz's* Wicked Witch of the West). Spy novelist Helen MacInnes, 77. Roger Maris, 51 (who in '61.hit a one-season record 61 home runs). Popster Ricky ("Travelin' Man") Nelson, 45. Circusmaster John Ringling North, 81. Diet guru Nathan Pritikin, 69. Seismologist Charles Richter, 85 (deviser of the scale used to gauge earthquake intensity). Gambling authority John Scarne, 82. Simone Signoret, 64. Orson Welles, 70.

In taking their first precise measurements of the ozone layer over Antarctica, scientists discover a hole, the significance of which would become hotly debated. And from his office in the White House basement, a National Security Council aide is juggling two disparate covert operations: Shipping missiles to Iran to effect the release of Americans held hostage in Beirut by Tehran-backed terrorists, and supplying arms and funds to Nicaragua's contras despite a House prohibition on such aid. Complicated, but Oliver North, 41, is a can-do Marine.

The Palestinians who skyjacked TWA Flight 847 to Beirut told attendant ULI DERICKSON (with son MATTHEW, 7) to check passports and identify the Jews among the 152 passengers and crew. The German-born Derickson, 40, refused. After a 17-day siege, all aboard but sailor Robert Stethem were rescued.

CHRISTOPHER LITTLE

Designed as a hangover cure by pharmacist John Pemberton of Atlanta in 1886 (the launch year also of Dr Pepper), Coca-Cola changed its formula to sweeten sales. NEW COKE proved the Edsel of sodas; the old drink, renamed "Coca-Cola Classic," was brought back in just 10 weeks.

AL FRENI

OURAGAN
U DERICKSON

REO Speedwagon's "Can't Fight This Feeling" was topping the charts about the time London Mayor **PETER DONOGHUE** escorted **PRINCESS DIANA** through an arts complex (*above*). His Honor somehow did. Not so valiant: **PRINCE CHARLES,** who paused between chukkers to give Di a royal goose (and the rest of us a saucy gander).

RON GALELLA (TOP LEFT); ROBIN NUNN (TOP RIGHT)

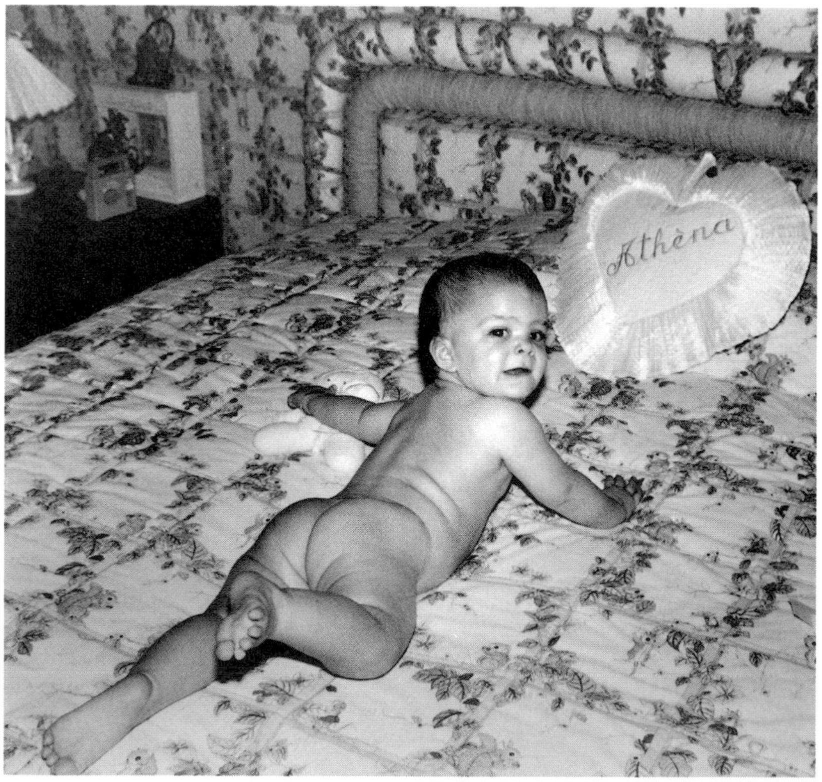

ATHINA ROUSSEL, 11 months, would never have to worry about her assets being bared. Dad Thierry Roussel, 31, was the scion of a French industrialist. More to the point, Mom Christina Onassis Bolker Andreadis Kauzov Roussel, 33, was sole heir to the shipping fortune built by her late father Aristotle. Yet the baby's life was soon darkened by divorce (Thierry accepted a $1.4-million-a-year settlement) and death (Christina accidentally OD'd on diet pills and tranquilizers in 1988). But in 2003, on reaching 18, Athina will become a billionairess.

CHRISTOS KORONTZIS / SCOOP / GAMMA-LIAISON

Forty-nine years after Anita Colby became the first model to command $100 an hour, **PAULINA PORIZKOVA,** 20, was billing $3,500 a day (on every day of the year once she signed a five-year, $6 million deal with Estée Lauder). Off-camera Paulina was seeing rocker Ric Ocasek, 36, of the Cars, whom she had met while taping the group's *Drive* video; they married in 1989 and had their first child four years later.

NEAL PRESTON

Other 300-pound linemen had chuffed across the NFL's gridirons; but as **LATAVIA PERRY,** 3, would attest, none had the easy charm of her dad, **WILLIAM (THE REFRIGERATOR),** 23. Madison Avenue agreed, paying the $340,000-a-year rookie another $750,000 or so to pitch comestibles like Big Macs and Coke. Oh, yes, Fridge won a Super Bowl ring his first year with the Chicago Bears, for whom he played nine seasons before signing with the Philadelphia Eagles.

ROBERT ROSAMILIO / NEW YORK DAILY NEWS

When it yapped out the car window at a drive-through, the waitress screamed and burst into tears. But **TWIGGY** was no *Gremlin,* just a 4-pound Chinese Crested (whose pinkish bodies are hairless and heavily warted) that was crowned Long Beach, California's Ugliest Dog.

JAVIER MENDOZA / LOS ANGELES HERALD EXAMINER

Nine years after ridding herself of Ike, **TINA TURNER,** 45, celebrated her MTV Best Female Video award for *What's Love Got To Do With It?* with an equally wigged-out **CHER.** Turner also grabbed four Grammys for her first solo No. 1, but for some reason Oscar chose to snub her hair-raising turn opposite Mel Gibson in *Mad Max: Beyond the Thunderdome.*

ROBIN PLATZER / TWIN IMAGES

When Ronald Reagan railed against "welfare queens," San Diego mom-on-the-dole **WHOOPI GOLDBERG** didn't take it personally; she just got her improv-honed act together and took it on the road. Two years later, Goldberg, 35, had a hit one-woman Broadway show as well as the lead in *The Color Purple,* the Steven Spielberg movie of novelist Alice Walker's 1983 Pulitzer Prizewinner.

ROGER RESSMEYER / STARLIGHT

So what if her voice was likened to "Minnie Mouse on helium." With MTV giving her new *Material Girl* saturation play and *Desperately Seeking Susan* giving her big-screen time as well, **MADONNA,** 26, was selling 75,000 vinyl discs per day. She also bade adieu to a new beau (who later briefly became her husband), Sean Penn, 24, for a concert swing that in New York City (*below*) left fan **JOHN F. KENNEDY JR.,** 24, white knuckled.

KEN REGAN / CAMERA 5 (RIGHT); DAVID McGOUGH / DMI

Thanks to the owners of the New Orleans eatery K-Paul's, Kay Hinrich and her husband **PAUL PRUDHOMME,** Louisiana enhanced its rep for great grub. The 13th child of a sharecropper, Chef Paul (left), the inventor of blackened redfish, was also hymning the glories of spicy Cajun and Creole dishes in a best-selling cookbook. All that work had slimmed him too, from a 500-pound teen to, at 44, a svelte 400-plus.

RAEANNE RUBENSTEIN

Whatever caused socialite Sunny von Bulow to lapse into an irreversible coma at her Newport, Rhode Island, estate in 1979, it wasn't husband **CLAUS.** Or so declared the second jury to try von Bulow, 58. (The first had convicted him in 1982 of injecting her with insulin, but legal scholar Alan Dershowitz won a reversal of fortune.)

TERRY SMITH

Lovers for a dozen years, **ANJELICA HUSTON,** 34, and **JACK NICHOLSON,** 48, costarred for the first time in her director father John's Mafia comedy *Prizzi's Honor*. It was also the last; by the time of their separate grease-painted smashes (she as Morticia Addams, he as Batman's nemesis, The Joker), Nicholson had sired his first child, with young actress Rebecca Broussard, and Huston had married sculptor Robert Graham.

HARRY BENSON

Elizabeth Taylor, Doris Day and Gina Lollabrigida on the big screen, Susan Saint James and Linda Evans on TV—**ROCK HUDSON** always had a way with the women. Not in real life. Though his homosexuality was no secret in the industry (in the mid-'50s, Universal pressured him into a sham marriage), it was to fans, until Hudson became the first star to confirm that he had AIDS. Two months and six days later, the actor, born Roy Fitzgerald in Winnetka, Illinois, was dead at 59.

CHUCK BANKUTI / SHOOTING STAR

Like Alex Keaton, his *Family Ties* proto-yup, **MICHAEL J. FOX** had the world on a short leash. The 24-year-old Canadian was driving not only prime-time's No. 2 show but also an odd couple of box-office hits: the filmed-on-the-fly *Teen Wolf* and the slick-as-Marty-McFly *Back to the Future.* If he kept up that bullish pace, the actor would be able to afford a studio of his very own by the time he became a 21st Century Fox.

TONY COSTA / OUTLINE

"Please check your egos at the door," read the placard at the entrance to an L.A. studio. Forty-five stars of rock, pop and country did just that—and also waived all royalties—to join a 9 p.m.-to-dawn session, initiated by Harry Belafonte and producer Ken Kragen and directed by Quincy Jones, to aid Ethiopian famine victims. Among those lending voice to the American version of Band Aid was that project's moving force, Bob Geldof, as well as (*back row, from left):* **DARYL HALL, STEVE PERRY, KENNY LOGGINS, JEFFREY OSBORNE** (*partly hidden)* and **LINDSEY BUCKINGHAM;** (*middle)* **AL JARREAU, DIONNE WARWICK, LIONEL RICHIE, KENNY ROGERS, HUEY LEWIS, BOB DYLAN, JOHN OATES** and **RUTH POINTER;** (*front)* **CYNDI LAUPER, BRUCE SPRINGSTEEN, JAMES INGRAM, SMOKEY ROBINSON, RAY CHARLES** and **SHEILA E.** The "We Are the World" single (cowritten by Richie and Michael Jackson), the follow-up *USA for Africa* LP and assorted United Support from Artists for Africa paraphernalia brought in nearly $50 million.

HENRY DILTZ / WE ARE THE WORLD

On January 28, seeking to "slip the surly bonds of Earth," they roared aloft aboard the *Challenger* (clockwise from *bottom left):* **MICHAEL SMITH,** 40, **ELLISON ONIZUKA,** 39; teacher **CHRISTA McAULIFFE,** 37; **GREGORY JARVIS,** 41; **JUDITH RESNIK,** 36; **RONALD McNAIR,** 35; and **FRANCIS SCOBEE,** 46. Seventy-four seconds later, with the shuttle already nine miles high, a $900 gasket in its right booster ruptured. At least four astronauts survived the fireball —but not the shattering impact, some four minutes later, of their craft against the unyielding waters of the Atlantic.

NASA

1986

How safe is the space shuttle? Chances of a catastrophic failure, NASA likes to boast, are one in 100,000. But after the program's 25th launch — the *Challenger* — the agency shortens the odds to one in 78 (not much different from the top card of a fresh deck being the queen of spades). Technological breakdowns, however, respect no national borders. A meltdown at the Soviet nuclear plant at Chernobyl, near Kiev, kills 31 and releases radioactive fallout that drifts across Europe as far north as Norway. Halley's Comet does reappear on schedule, but its glow is bright only in Chile (next visit: 2061).

Hawaii's newest immigrants are the Marcoses of Manila, forced to flee the Philippines they had ironfistedly ruled for 20 years. After Ferdinand, 68, rigs the count of his presidential race against Corazon Aquino, 53, the widow of assassinated dissident Benigno, Filipinos vote again with protest marches, bottles and rocks (even without yet knowing that Imelda, 54, had managed to afford 4,500 pairs of shoes on her husband's $5,700 salary). Austrians prove more forgiving. Though evidence suggests that one seeker of high office, former U.N. Secretary General Kurt Waldheim, 67, was guilty of World War II crimes against Jews, he trots out the Joe Isuzu defense ("Trust me") and wins the presidency.

Dick Rutan, 48, and Jeana Yeager, 34, fly around the world in nine days without stopping or refueling. Impressive though the 20.8 mpg achieved by their plastic-and-paper craft is. it doesn't wow Detroit, whose gas-efficiency champ wrings out 58 highway mpg: Chevrolet's (made-in-Japan) Sprint ER.

What do you call nine attorneys up to their necks in sand? Not enough sand. What do you call nine attorneys up to their necks in back-stabbing, lechery and goofball cases? The partners and associates of McKenzie, Brachman, Chaney and Kuzak, practitioners of *L.A. Law;* the series' Nielsens, though, would take awhile to catch up with its critical acclaim.

Passages: Paperback Gothic queen V.C. Andrews, 62. Outdoors-wearman Eddie Bauer, 86. Argentine author Jorge Luis Borges, 86. Jimmy Cagney, 86. Swing King Benny Goodman, 77. Cary Grant, 80. Candido Jacuzzi, 83 (who in 1949, to soothe a son suffering from rheumatoid arthritis, cobbled together a heated whirlpool bath). Industrial design guru Raymond Loewy, 93. Author Bernard Malamud, 71. Painter Georgia O'Keeffe, 98. Admiral Hyman Rickover, 86 (who nuclear-powered the U.S. Navy). Tenzing Norkay, 72 (who in 1953 led Edmund Hillary to the crest of Mount Everest). TV zooman Marlin Perkins, 81. Wallis Simpson Warfield, the Duchess of Windsor, 89 (the twice-divorced American for whom Edward VIII abdicated the British throne in 1936).

Former National Security Adviser Bud McFarlane, 48, and Oliver North sneak into Tehran bearing gifts (spare missile parts, six pistols and a chocolate cake) but leave without securing the release of a single Mideast hostage. Only when an unmarked C-47 cargo plane is brought down over the jungles of Nicaragua by Sandinista ground fire — and surviving American mercenary Eugene Hasenfus, 45, starts talking — does Iran-contra begin to unravel. And bringing down the ceilings at Cole High School in San Antonio, Texas, is a new student, an Air Force brat who at 14 stands 6'9": Shaquille O'Neal.

.V____ ___T_. (On TV's most popular game show, contestants twirled the *Wheel of Fortune* and tried to fill in the blanks.) V____ _H_T_. (Because vowels paid nothing, everybody concentrated on guessing consonants.) V____ WH_T_. (A correct guess filling more than one slot paid extra.) V_NN_ WH_T_. (At the board turning the tiles: VANNA WHITE, 29, whose $100,000-plus salary for a task as easy as A-B-C struck some as D-U-H; yet host Pat Sajak's duties weren't exactly brain surgery either.)

CHARLES BUSH / SHOOTING STAR

Reno, Nevada's **GREG LeMOND,** 25, left 50 million Frenchmen feeling quite Huffy: On Day 23 of the 83rd Tour de France, with native son and defending champ Bernard Hinault a scant 190 seconds behind, he biked across the finish line to become the first Yank to win the 2,542-mile race.

Her third and latest bust was for protesting campus recruitment by the CIA, which used to report to her father. But just as Dad was no longer President, **AMY CARTER** was no longer First Daughter, just another 19-year-old Brown University sophomore.

RAEANNE RUBENSTEIN

BETTE MIDLER looked divine because she had recently: a) seen her first comedy LP, *Mud Will Be Flung,* make the charts; b) turned 40; c) celebrated one year of marriage to commodities broker Harry Kipper, 37; d) read reviews of her comeback movie, *Down and Out in Beverly Hills;* e) all of the above.

HARRY BENSON

Onscreen, **CLINT EASTWOOD** was refighting the invasion of Grenada in *Heartbreak Ridge.* Offscreen, he was bearing armfuls of babies in his quest for elected office. Easily whupping Carmel, California's incumbent mayor (62-year-old former librarian Charlotte Townsend), Eastwood, 55, then made his own day by firing the officials who had denied him a building permit.

GARY PARKER / SAN JOSE MERCURY NEWS / BLACK STAR

Two years after her star-crossed '84 Olympics, the intense **MARY DECKER SLANEY,** 27, was far more mellow thanks to second husband **BRIAN SLANEY,** 30, a British discus thrower, and their first child, **ASHLEY.** She competed again at Seoul in 1988, finishing credibly in the metric mile and the 3,000 meter, but failed in her bid to qualify for the 1992 U.S. Olympic team.

NEAL PRESTON

In a display of noblesse oblige, the royal known as Randy Andy and his high-spirited fiancée both invited ex-lovers to their wedding. **PRINCE ANDREW** and **SARAH FERGUSON**, both 26, had two daughters before photos surfaced of Fergie topless on the Riviera, putting her foot not in her own mouth but that of American John Bryan. The Yorks divorced in 1993.

KEN GOFF

TATUM O'NEAL, 22, took as her husband tennis champion **JOHN McENROE**, 27, and soon started a family that would grow to three children. But there was bad news to bear in 1992; the couple decided to separate, in part because he was opposed to her desire to resume acting.

ANTHONY SAVIGNANO / RON GALELLA

BARBARA WALTERS, 53, and Lorimar chairman **MERV** (*Dallas, Knots Landing*) **ADELSON**, 55, exchanged vows, each for the third time (flanked by, from *left*, attendant **AMANDA GOLDBERG**; his daughter **ELLIE BAILEY**; her daughter **JACQUELINE**; and his sons **GARY** and **ANDY**). But opposite-coast careers proved irreconcilable; they were divorced in 1992.

PETER BORSARI

After an eight-year courtship, telejournalist **MARIA** (*CBS Morning News*) **SHRIVER**, 30, wed action star **ARNOLD SCHWARZENEGGER**, 38, on Cape Cod (she came from the Massachusetts Kennedys; he campaigned for Ronald Reagan). Their third child and first son was born in 1993.

CHRISTOPHER LITTLE

Law student **CAROLINE KENNEDY,** 28, was escorted by Uncle **TED** to her altar rendezvous with Manhattan artist and design-firm president Edwin Schlossberg, 42 (who bonded with his future in-laws by way of a prenuptial game of touch football). The couple's third child and first son was born in 1993.

MIKE FULLER

The first time Mötley Crüe drummer **TOMMY LEE** telephoned **HEATHER** (*T.J. Hooker, Dynasty*) **LOCKLEAR** to chat, she quickly realized that he had her mixed up with another TV blonde named Heather (Thomas of *The Fall Guy).* No matter; less than a year later, the small-screen beauty, 24, and the heavy-metal beast, 23, were walking down the aisle (outfitted more conventionally than in the pre-wedding shot at left; she wanted her gown to remain a surprise). They separated in late 1993.

NEAL PRESTON

One guess whose first LP featured a track titled "I Can't Live Without My Radio." Correct, it was **L.L. COOL J,** the nom de rap of 18-year-old James Todd Smith of Queens, New York. With album sales reaching 600,000 and Hollywood calling (he contributed the title song to Goldie Hawn's gridiron comedy, *Wildcats),* Cool J no longer needed a boombox to signal his arrival.

ANDY LEVIN

Most pop divas had the arrogance of Maria Callas but the pipes of Betty Boop. Not **WHITNEY HOUSTON,** 23, whose octave-hopping sincerity powered the hit single "Saving All My Love for You" and made her debut album, *Whitney Houston,* the year's top, with sales of 7 million-plus. So was anyone surprised that when it came time for her to hire a *Bodyguard,* he would be Kevin Costner?

STEVEN MEISEL

Whether ferreting out Commies for Senator Joe McCarthy in the '50s or mouthpiecing for a rogue's gallery of wealthy clients, lawyer **ROY COHN** didn't mind leaving bruises. Thus, few mourned when the IRS seized his assets, and New York State disbarred him, shortly before Cohn's death at 60, of AIDS.

HARRY BENSON

In his 35th year, **STEVIE WONDER** played some fresh songs in the key of life. He composed an estimated 300 new tunes; released his twentysomethingth album; won his 16th Grammy; launched a 50-state tour; and even made light of his blindness by posing for an anti-alcohol poster that read: "Before I ride with a drunk, I'll drive myself."

NEAL PRESTON

Five years after **KEITH HARING,** 28, started to chalk up New York City subway stations with the stick squiggles that soon became his trademark (*left*), he was fetching as much as $42,500 a canvas, designing Swatch faces and even executing a 110-yard-long, 14-foot-high mural on the Berlin Wall. Haring's naive motifs continued to sell after his death of AIDS in 1990.

VLADIMIR SICHOV / SIPA PRESS

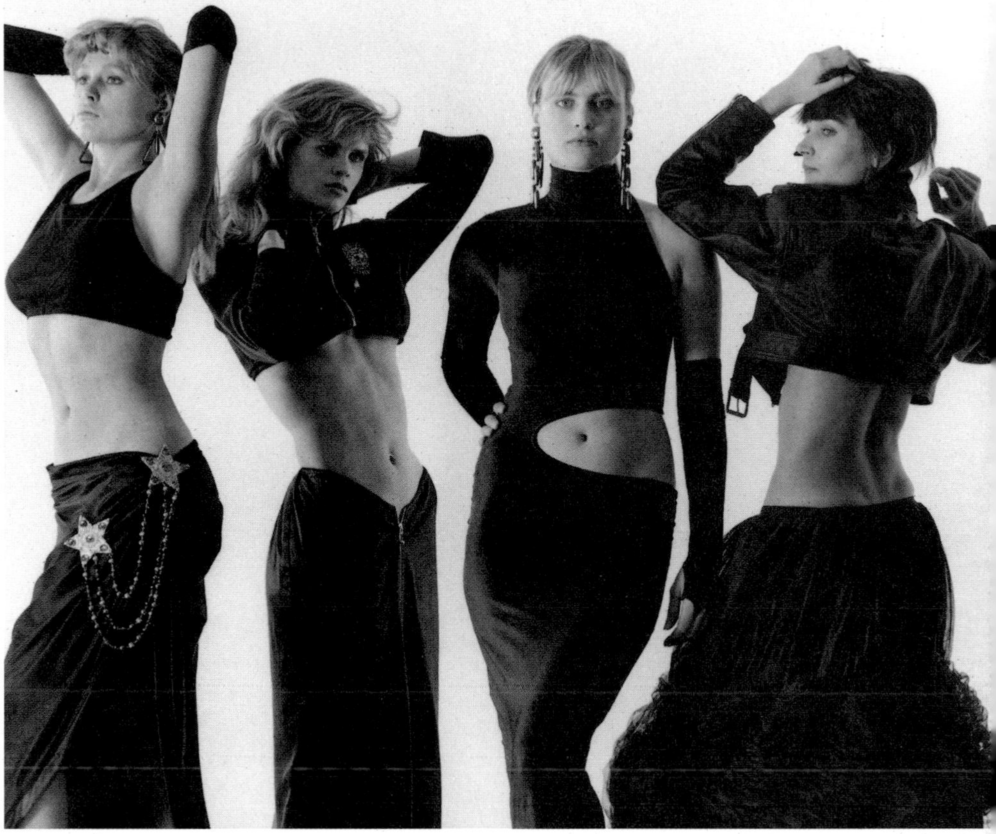

Forget Annapolis; the trendy navel academy was situated in Manhattan's garment district, whose designers were betting that the Soloflex set wanted to showcase their **BARE MIDRIFFS.** The fashion was not only a treat for innie- and outie-admirers but also a free billboard for tummy-tuckers and liposuctionists.

CO RENTMEESTER

As those annoying ads kept reminding us, prunes were not funny. Except to the writers of *Golden Girls,* NBC's smash new geriatricom (on which hot flashes, not-so-hot senior bed partners and adult diapers were all grist for giggles). The show's stars, from near right: **BETTY WHITE,** 63; **BEA ARTHUR**, 61; and **RUE McCLANAHAN,** 51. (Estelle Getty, 62, must have been off raiding the fridge for more Sunsweet.)

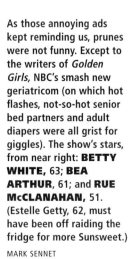

MARK SENNET

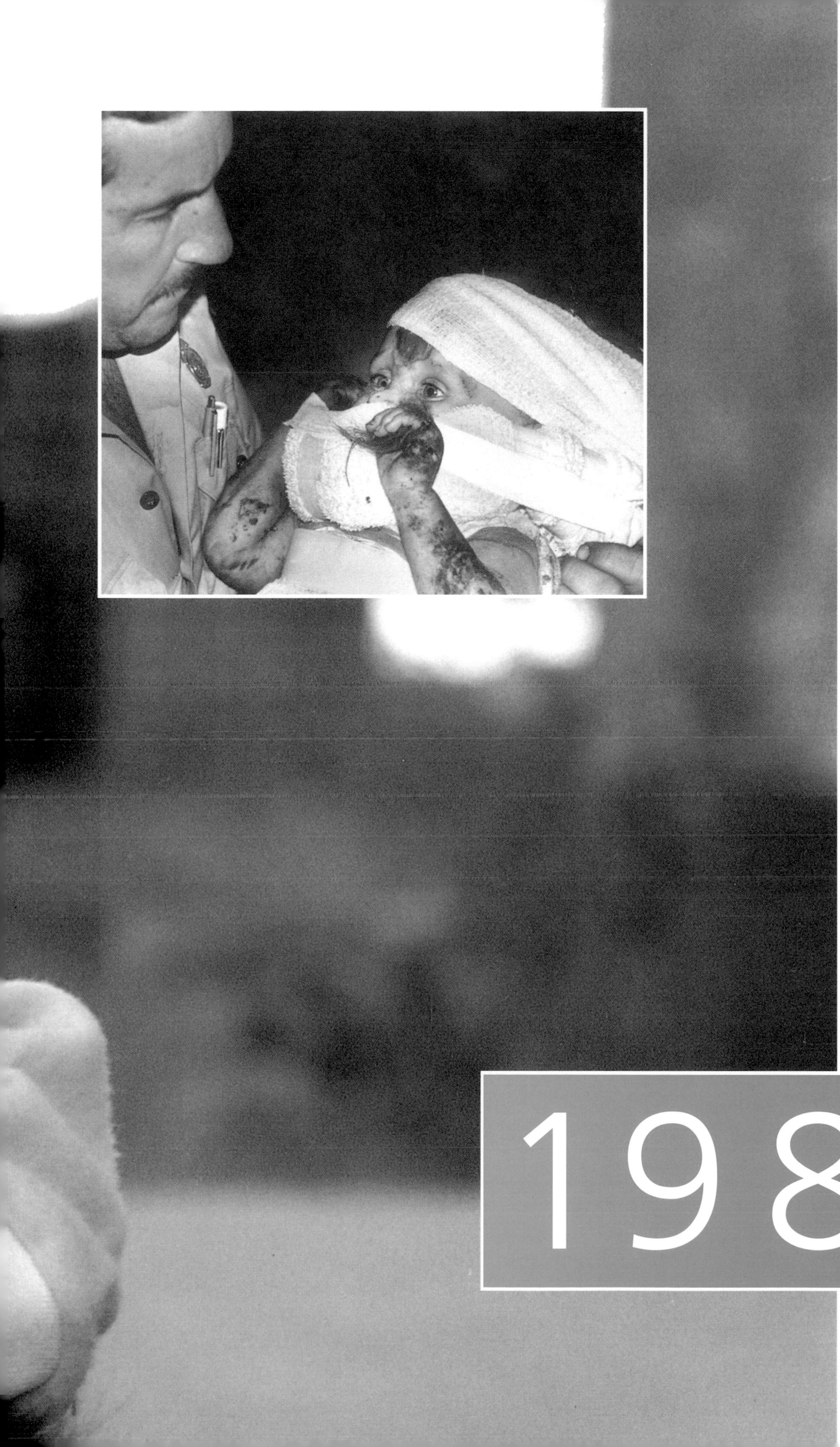

1987

JESSICA McCLURE of Midland, Texas, earned her sunshine-bright smile the hard way—by surviving 58 hours of hellish darkness. On a Wednesday morning in October, the 18-month-old tumbled down an abandoned well too narrow for an adult to enter. As the nation held its breath, a volunteer army that grew to 450 had to drill through granite to sink a parallel shaft. By the time the resilient Jessica was lifted to safety (*inset*) on live TV, nobody seemed to mind that the uncapped well sat in the backyard of her aunt's unlicensed toddler center.

JOE McNALLY;
SCOTT SHAW / SIPA PRESS (INSET)

United Nations statisticians calculate that with the birth of a boy named Matej Gaspar in Yugoslavia, the world's population reaches 5 billion (previous benchmarks: 1 billion in 1801; 2 billion in 1925; 3 billiion in 1959; 4 billion in 1974). Big numbers seem the norm. Ronald Reagan submits America's first trillion-dollar budget, which passes. Nine months after the Dow-Jones breaks the 2000 barrier, the market bungee-jumps 508 points; yet Black Monday's paper losses of $500 billion would be recouped before decade's end. And the income tax return filed by junk-bond whiz Michael Milken, 40, shows that he received from Drexel Burnham Lambert total compensation of $550 million, or roughly triple the gross national product of Grenada.

In the USSR, Mikhail Gorbachev finds time while promoting *glasnost* (openness) and *perestroika* (economic reconstruction) to oust his Air Defense Minister and the Moscow Communist Party head. The first had allowed West German teenager Matthias Rust to pilot a single-engine Cessna through 700 miles of Soviet air space and land it smack in the middle of Red Square. The second was merely insubordinate; but such is the style of 56-year-old Boris Yeltsin.

Gary Hart's style is revealed in a published snapshot that shows model Donna Rice, 29, on the lap of the married senator who had been, until then, the front-runner for his party's 1988 presidential nomination. Conversely, fellow Democrat Barney Frank, 47, becomes the first Representative to publicly acknowledge his homosexuality, yet would win re-election the following year.

Television produces a pair of unlikely cliff-hangers. Would Yale Law School professor Robert Bork, 60, survive his contentious Senate Judiciary Committee hearings and win a seat on the Supreme Court? (No.) Would televangelist Oral Roberts, 69, who confides that the Lord will "call him home" unless viewers call in $4.5 million, meet his Maker? (Not yet.) Elsewhere, the California Raisins put a fresh wrinkle on commercials by covering a Marvin Gaye hit, and the brie-and-chablis set acquires the taste for a new white whine: ABC's *thirtysomething*.

Passages: Cellist Jacqueline DuPré, 42. German-born physicist Klaus Fuchs, 76 (whose 1950 conviction for selling British atomic secrets to the USSR led to the arrest in America of Julius and Ethel Rosenberg). Jackie Gleason, 71. Rita Hayworth, 68. Violinist Jascha Heifitz, 86. Defecting Nazi Rudolf Hess, 93 (jailed since 1947 at Berlin's Spandau Prison, the last 20 years as the lone inmate; by his own hand). Moviemaker John Huston, 81. Liberace, 68. Lee Marvin, 63. Sociologist Gunnar Myrdal, 88. Maria von Trapp, 82 (whose family's adventures in Austria just before the Nazi occupation inspired *The Sound of Music).*

Who needs vaudeville and *Star Search* when there are so many shopping malls around? Two veterans of the galleria circuit graduate to the national charts: Los Angeles' Tiffany ("I Think We're Alone Now"), 16, and Long Island's Debby ("Electric Youth") Gibson, 18. It also smells like teen spirit in Aberdeen, Washington, where punk-rock-aficionado buddies Kurt Cobain, 18, and Chris Novoselic, 22, decide to try making music themselves; they name their group Nirvana. And back in Boston, schoolmates Evan Dando, Ben Deily and Jesse Peretz, all 20, release "Hate Your Friends," their first LP as the Lemonheads.

Budweiser had the Clydesdales on tap, but they seemed too plodding to pitch a beer aimed at the Light crowd. Enter SPUDS McKENZIE. How did the Party Animal keep cool in the midst of those crowds of bikinied nubilities? Perhaps because like Lassie, Honey Tree Evil Eye was also a she (the English bullterrier died in 1993 at age 10).

PETER SERLING

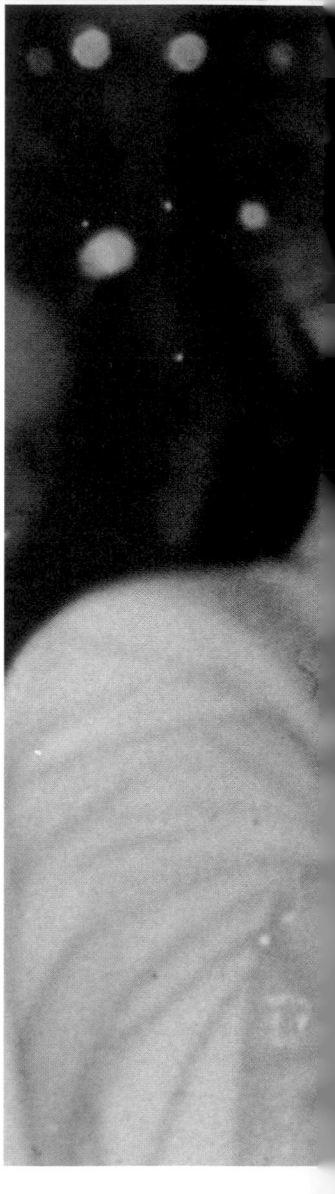

Handed a prop bottle of champagne on a London movie set, PRINCESS DIANA couldn't resist uncorking a bit of brut force on PRINCE CHARLES. Despite a less-than-bubbly buzz from the British tabloids, the Waleses were still, to all outward appearances, very much a royal couple.

ALPHA / GLOBE

First, there was *Kukla, Fran & Ollie.* Now it was Iran-contra, Fawn & Ollie, in which a House panel probing the rococo arms-for-hostages deal treated paper-shredding secretary **FAWN HALL,** 27 (*top right),* with kid gloves and beat a hasty retreat before *semper fi* Marine **OLIVER NORTH,** 43 (who pinned the blame on his mentor, the late CIA director William Casey).

STANLEY TRETICK (TOP RIGHT); HARRY BENSON

At 41, having leveraged his dad's $25 million in Brooklyn and Queens rental properties into a Manhattan real estate-and-Atlantic City-casino empire valued by aides at $3 billion, **DONALD TRUMP** shared some tips in his best-selling *The Art of the Deal.* But by the 1990 sequel, The Donald (as Czech-born wife No. 1, **IVANA,** 37, called him) was fending off creditors while wooing wife No.2-to-be, Marla Maples, 23.

HARRY BENSON

JESSICA HAHN, 28, said she had been a pious church secretary when PTL minister Jim Bakker and a male aide holy-rollered her into bed in 1980, then offered her $265,000 to keep the faith. She didn't. Not only did her below-the-Bible-Belt revelations force Jim and Tammy Faye Bakker to say amen to televangelism but they also set Hahn on a second career: *Playboy* model and 1-900 sex-line hostess.

HARRY BENSON

Who unloosed the libidinous Church Lady on TV? Could it be . . . Satan? Nope, just *Saturday Night Live,* which added to the flood tide of gospel shows by creating one for purse-lipped **DANA CARVEY,** 32. Well, isn't she special? Yup, as were Carvey's later dead-on send-ups of George Bush and Ross Perot, plus his bohemian-rhapsodizing Garth, the hunk that stole *Wayne's World.* (*Not!*)

NBC

At 79, **BETTE DAVIS** published *This 'n That,* her second best-seller, and made *The Whales of August,* her 100th movie (and first since surviving a mastectomy and a stroke four years earlier). She was also lobbying to star in Hollywood's adaptation of a new off-Broadway play. Davis's instincts were unerring; though she died in 1989, the year of that picture's release, *Driving Miss Daisy* won Jessica Tandy an Oscar.

TONY COSTA / OUTLINE

The **RAY** brothers—**RANDY,** 8 (in striped shirt), **ROBBY,** 9 (*top right)* and **RICKY,** 10—were hemophiliacs who had tested HIV positive. Parents Cliff and Louise, who with daughter Candy, 6, were uninfected, had their sons home-tutored for a year, then sued to allow them to attend public school. Less than three months later, the family's house burned down. The Rays finally resettled near Orlando. Ricky died in 1992, by which time his brothers also had full-blown AIDS.

GARTH FRANCIS / FORT MYERS NEWS PRESS

Will the last person to leave Lake Wobegon please turn off the lights? Minnesota humorist **GARRISON KEILLOR,** 45, did just that by moving from his native St. Paul to New York City. But five years later he went home again to resume sharing the daily life of the imaginary hamlet so deftly limned on National Public Radio's *A Prairie Home Companion* and in three best-sellers.

KEVIN HORAN

The night in 1983 when *A Chorus Line* broke Broadway's longevity record with performance No. 3,389, its creator, **MICHAEL BENNETT,** shared a bow with 322 past and present cast members. On July 2, just before the curtain rose on performance No. 4,958, Broadway dimmed its lights for one minute in honor of the showman, who had succumbed to AIDS-related cancer at 44.

ROBIN PLATZER / TWIN IMAGES

With a daughter in common, it wasn't as if the couple hadn't spoken in the decade since their split. Still, **SONNY** and **CHER** had a lot to catch up on in a late-night reunion. At 52, he was now a Bono fide political candidate (for mayor of Palm Springs, California). And at 41, she was now an actress (latest movie: *Moonstruck,* which also pretty much sums up host **DAVID LETTERMAN**).

NBC

Hollywood's Victim of the Year—and its Raptor of the Year—were both portrayed by **MICHAEL DOUGLAS,** 43. In *Fatal Attraction*, his naive one-night-standee was stalked by Glenn Close to a hare-braising finale. And in *Wall Street,* his greed-is-good arbitrageur was a fount of acid Yuphorisms ("Want a friend? Buy a dog"). Either way, the time seemed ripe for a gentler, kinder America.

TERRY O'NEILL / SYGMA

Bad was **MICHAEL JACKSON**'s first LP in five years. It was also how he felt about renewed rumors concerning his use of skin bleachers (denied) and his resort to plastic surgery (yes, but only the nose and chin). Touring in Japan (*below*), the press-shy singer, 29, released a handwritten response (*right*) as unsettling as his 1987 bid for the real-life Elephant Man's remains.

NEAL PRESTON (BELOW)

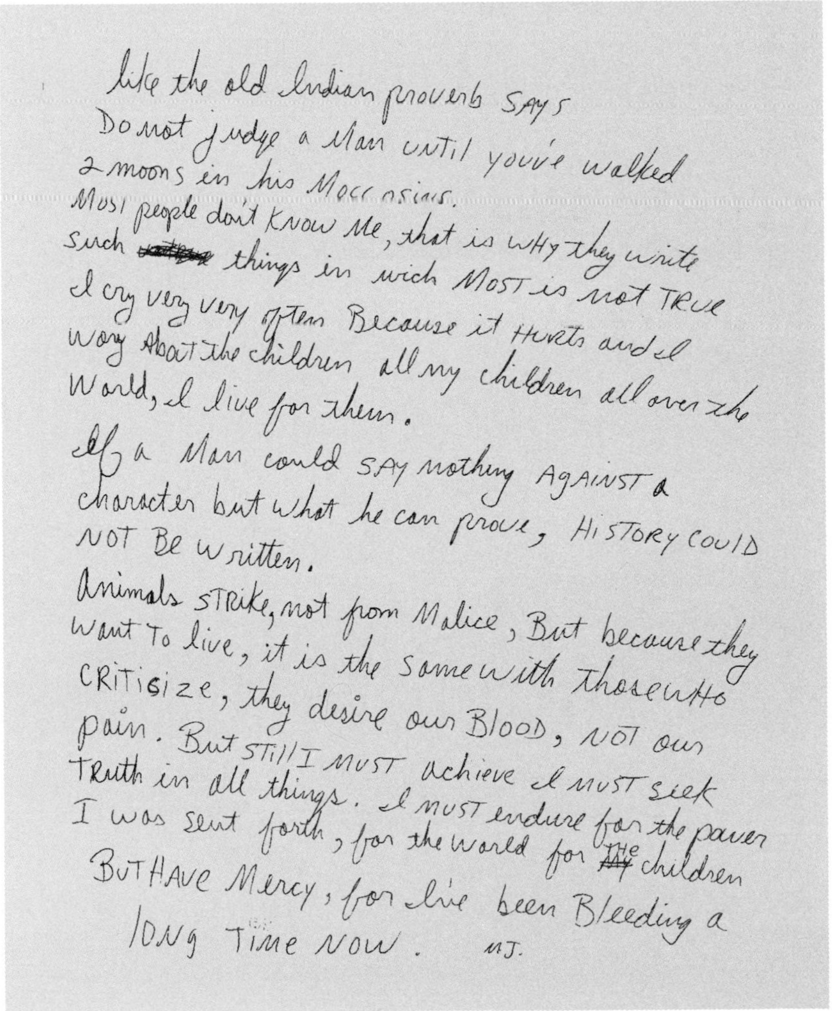

like the old Indian proverb SAys
Do not judge a Man until you've walked
2 moons in his Moccasins.
Most people don't Know Me, that is wHy they write
such ~~things~~ things in wich MOST is not TRUE
I cry very very often Because it Hurts and I
wory About the children all my children all over the
World, I live for them.
If a Man could SAy nothing AGAINST a
character but what he can prove, HiSTORy COULD
NOT Be written.
Animals STRike, not from Malice, But because they
Want To live, it is the Same with those WHO
CRITiSize, they desire our BLOOD, NOT our
pain. But STILL I MUST achieve I MUST SEEK
TRuth in all things. I MUST endure for the power
I was sent forth, for the world for THE children
BUT HAVE Mercy, for I've been Bleeding a
lONg TiMe NOW. MJ.

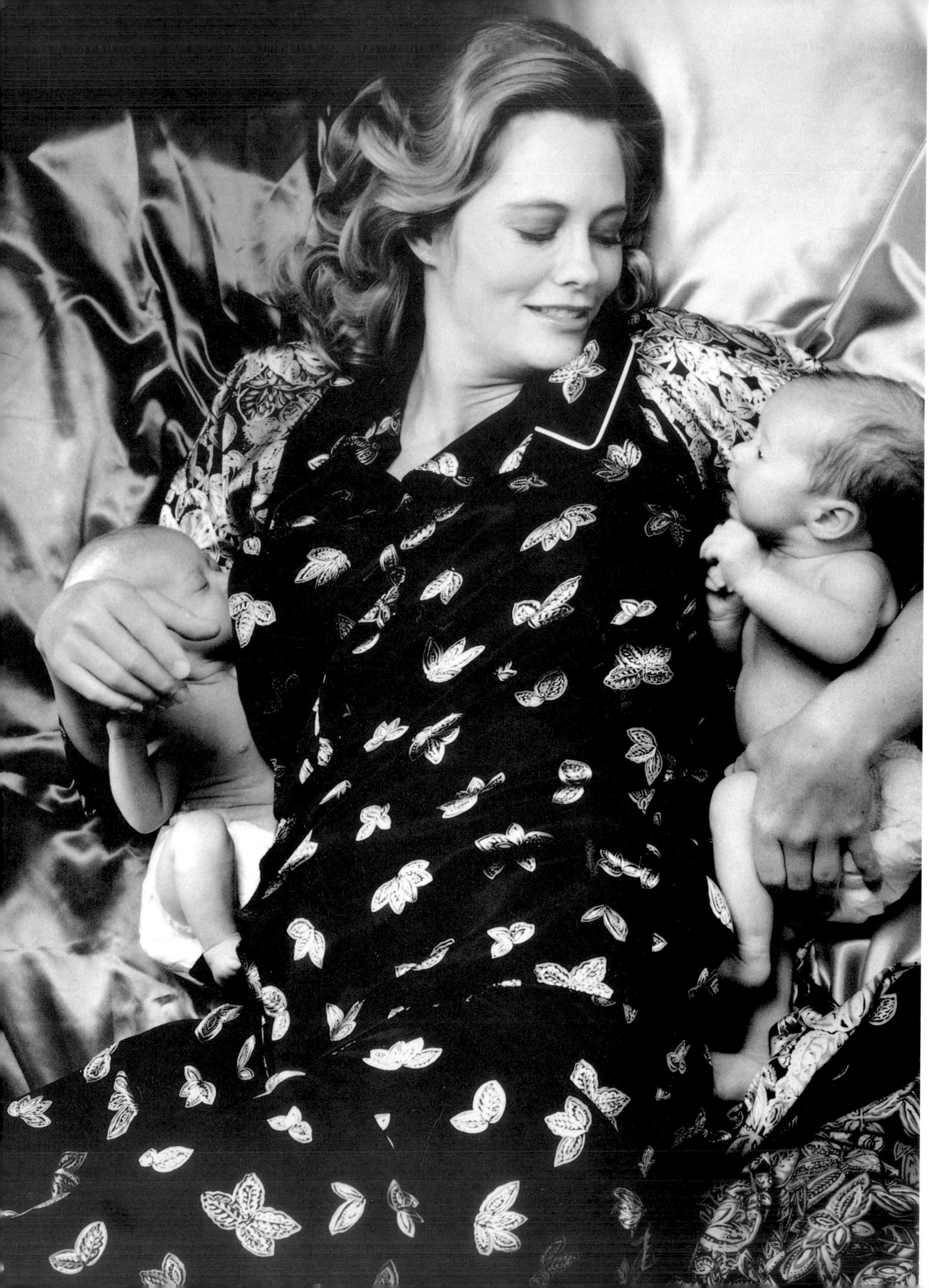

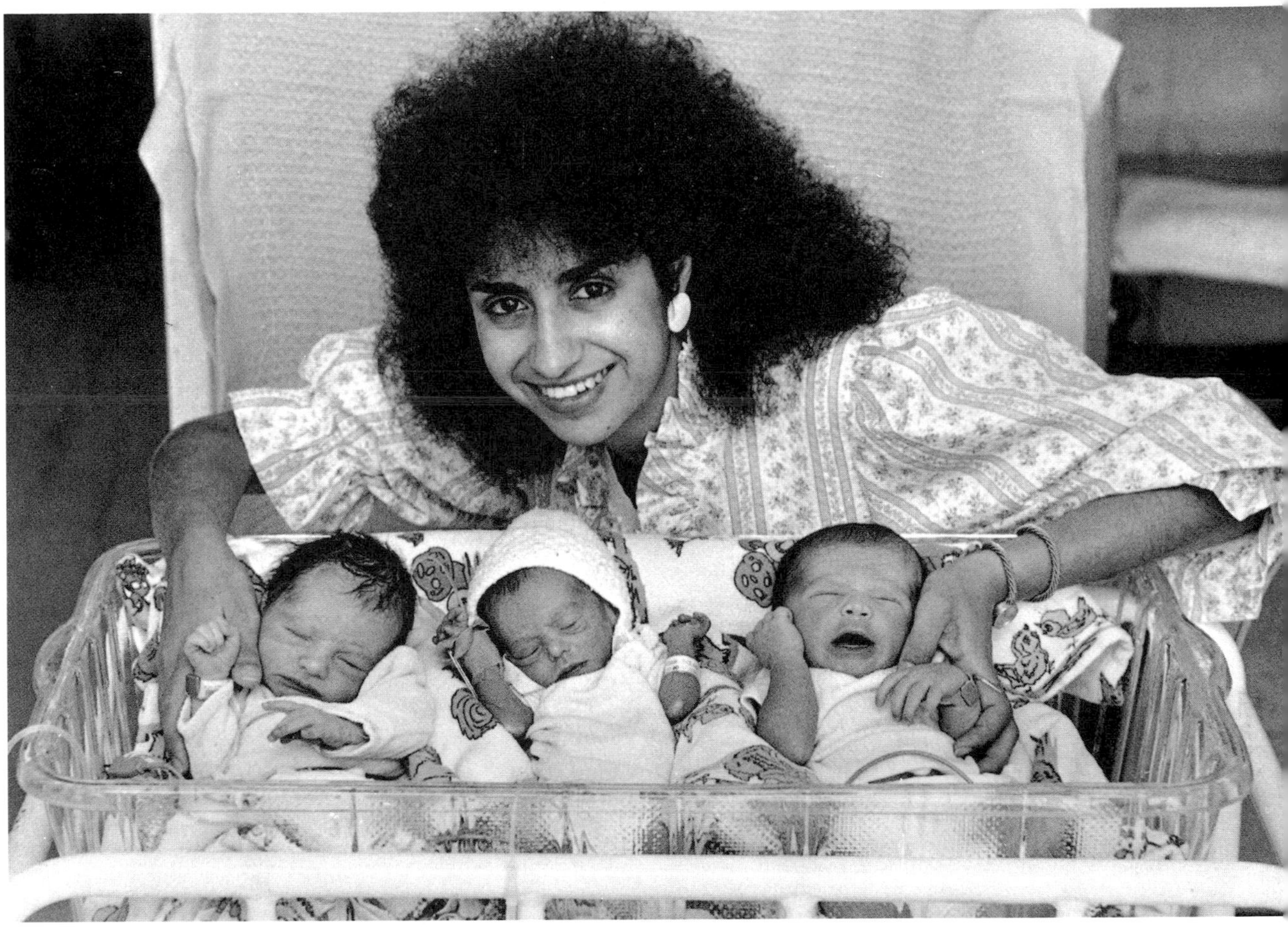

KAREN FERREIRA-JORGE, 25, of Tzaneen, South Africa, became the mother of (from *right)* **PAULA, JOSE** and **DAVID** even after her uterus had been removed following complications from her first pregnancy. Karen's eggs, fertilized in vitro by husband Alcino's sperm, were carried to term by a surrogate—her own Mom. Pat Anthony, 48, thus bore her own grandchildren; further, the triplets were both Karen's kids and also her siblings.

LYNN HILTON / DAVID O'NEILL / DAILY MAIL / SIPA PRESS

Blame the **SHEPHERD-OPPENHEIM** twins, **ARIEL** (*left)* and **ZACK,** for some of the backstage frictions that racked ABC's *Moonlighting.* Mom **CYBILL,** 37, who on learning her condition quickly wed husband No. 2, chiropractor Bruce Oppenheim, 39, had a difficult pregnancy that slowed production. The series folded the next year; Shepherd's marriage lasted until 1989.

TONY COSTA / OUTLINE

MIA FARROW, 42, often included her brood, which then numbered eight (five adopted, including Korean-born **SOON-YI PREVIN,** 16, *far right),* on dates with **WOODY ALLEN,** 51. But by the time Allen began filming 1992's *Husbands and Wives,* in which he revisited a theme from his 1979 *Manhattan (*middle-aged man smitten by teenage girl), he was trading pillow talk with not Mia but Soon-Yi.

DAVID McGOUGH / DMI

WINFREY
18
SWANN
88

1988

This was yo-yo dieting at its most public. To mark her five-month Optifast slim-down from jodhpur-thighed celeb softballer (*far left*) to size-10 syndicated star, **OPRAH WINFREY,** 36, dragged on stage a little red wagon heaped with 67 pounds of animal suet. Two years later, though, she hosted a show whose title sadly said it all: "The Pain of Regain." But don't turn that dial yet; by late 1993, Winfrey had spun back down into the buck-and-a-half range.

RAEANNE RUBENSTEIN (FAR LEFT); HARPO PRODUCTIONS

The men of the *USS Vincennes,* on patrol in the Persian Gulf, know they are in harm's way. Only 14 months earlier, 37 U.S. sailors died when the *USS Stark* was attacked by an Iraqi fighter (Saddam Hussein's apology was accepted). As an unidentified plane approaches it from Iran, the *Vincennes* opens fire. Tragically, the downed target is a scheduled Iran Air flight carrying 290 civilians. No such human error attends the destruction of Pan Am 103. Mideast-sponsored terrorists smuggle past security a plastique-filled cassette player that detonates over Lockerbie, Scotland, killing all 259 aboard the 747 and 11 villagers.

Yet elsewhere, peace is breaking out. Iraq and Iran call off their war after eight years and 1 million dead, with both combatants claiming a victory that is purely Pyrrhic. And Mikhail Gorbachev begins withdrawing Soviet troops from Afghanistan after nine years and 2 million-plus dead on both sides.

At the Seoul Olympics, Canada's Ben Johnson, 26, runs 100 meters in 9.79 seconds to become the world's fastest human on steroids (his mark is stricken, his medal stripped, his eligibility revoked). America continues its war on another drug when a federal grand jury indicts, in absentia, Manuel Noriega, 47, for cocaine smuggling. The Panamanian dictator shows no signs of surrendering.

Otherwise, the national mood seems to be summed up by the Bobby McFerrin hit, "Don't Worry, Be Happy." Roger and Jessica Rabbit hop atop the box-office charts while the Energizer Bunny (no relation) starts thumping its sponsor's virtues. Michelle Pfeiffer hits a trifecta: *Married to the Mob, Tequila Sunrise, Dangerous Liaisons* (OK, OK, *Tequila* did need some more salt). And just when you thought it was safe to throw out the joysticks for those old Atari and Coleco sets, along come Nintendo's Super Mario Brothers.

On the 3,838th and last carry of his 13-year pro football career, Chicago Bear running back Walter Payton, 33, hits the right side for five yards, extending his NFL best to 16,726 yards (or 9½ miles plus a first down or two). The contact sport of mergers and acquisitions also hits a milestone: the $25 billion deal for RJR Nabisco (a leveraged buyout later play-by-played in *Barbarians at the Gate*).

Passages: Cartoonist Charles Addams, 76. Raymond Carver, 50. Automaker Enzo Ferrari, 90. Physicist Richard Feynman, 69 (who at the 1986 *Challenger* hearings proved with a glass of ice water that the rubber-like O-ring gaskets become brittle when chilled; at the shuttle's launch, the temperature had been 38° Fahrenheit). Science fictionalist Robert Heinlein, 80. Amazon rain forest environmentalist Francisco "Chico" Mendes, 44 (murdered by area ranchers). Western novelist Louis L'Amour, 80. Sculptor and lanternmaker Isamu Noguchi, 84. Popster Roy ("Pretty Woman") Orbison, 52. South African novelist Alan (*Cry the Beloved Country*) Paton, 85. British-born Soviet spy Kim Philby, 76 (in Moscow). Caninologist Barbara (*No Bad Dog*) Woodhouse, 78.

Seeking to demonstrate his cyberspatial skills, hacker Robert Tappan Morris, 25, logs on to the global Internet and releases a virus that because of miscoding causes 6,000 computers to crash. He is fined $10,000 and given three year's probation — just the sort of arrogant egghead prank and mollycoddling treatment that Rush Limbaugh, 37, likes to decry on his new syndicated radio show.

His Diogenes-like search for an honest vote led Democratic presidential hopeful MICHAEL DUKAKIS into a West Virginia coal mine. The ex-Massachusetts governor, 55, was angered by a GOP attack ad rehashing Willie Horton (a rapist who killed while on prison furlough), yet froze at a debate when asked what he'd do if wife Kitty were raped. He and Lloyd Bentsen won 111 Electoral College votes.

STEVE LISS / TIME / ASSOCIATED PRESS

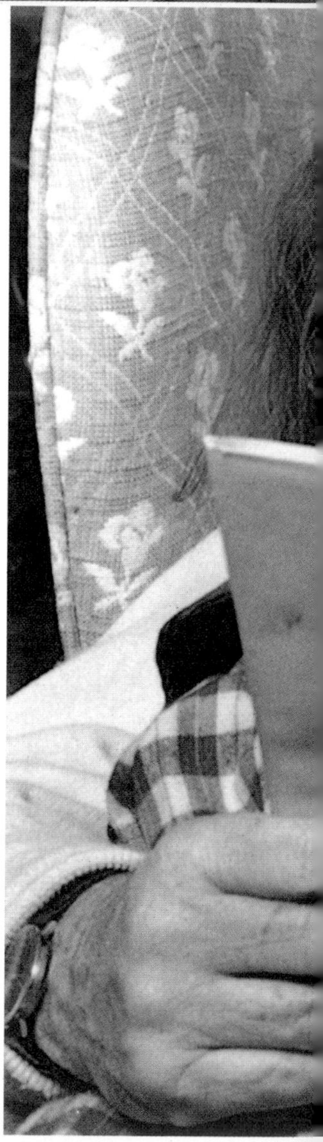

No, the tale being read to BARBARA *(near right)* and JENNA BUSH by their "Gampy" GEORGE wasn't *Bedtime for Bonzo,* but with Ronald Reagan at his two-term limit, it was time for Bush, 64, to run. Despite infelicitous phrases ("the vision thing") and the choice of an unheralded running mate, Bush and Dan Quayle, 41, won 426 Electoral College votes and the White House.

CHRISTOPHER LITTLE

Bea and Mr. Jones
Story and Pictures by Amy Schwartz

In *The Naked Gun,* the Gulden-boy cop played by **LESLIE NIELSEN,** 62, didn't know the meaning of the word fear (and probably couldn't spell it, either). The yukfest forever shattered the actor's typecasting as a stolid second lead, while proving that when it came to comedy, **PRISCILLA PRESLEY,** 42, also knew how to cut the mustard.

ELLIOTT MARKS

Gee, was it something **MORTON DOWNEY JR.** (*right*) said? At 55, he gave up trying to sing like his '30s crooner dad and built a TV talk show on his conservative bellicosity ("Zip it, pablum-puker!"). But the next year, after Downey claimed that skinheads had swastikaed his face, stations looked at his shrinking ad support and sent out a Mortifying order: "Get outta here!"

PETER SERLING

Presumably, **PHIL DONAHUE,** 52, didn't raid wife Marlo Thomas's closet when he found himself with nothing to wear to host an episode of his talk show devoted to transvestites. But the wardrobers of *Donahue* really let their boss down. Those over-the-calf socks? Tacky, tacky. And those flats? Oh, puh-*leese!*

ALAN SINGER

And the answer is: The Democratic Party mascot. Now, in this hermetically sealed envelope, the question: What animal was **JIMMY CARTER** good-naturedly emulating at a Colorado benefit for handicapped skiers when he performed a Carnak the Magnificent takeoff? Answer No. 2: Johnny Carson, Jay Leno, David Letterman. Question: Who didn't lose much sleep?

NATHAN BILOW / ASSOCIATED PRESS

The **L'ESPERANCE** babies—**ALEXANDRIA** (*near right*), **VERONICA, RAYMOND, DANIELLE** and **ERICA**—of Davis, Michigan, were America's first in-vitro quints. Their folks, luckily, were not first-time parents. Mom Michelle, 34, a model, had two boys before marrying dad Ray, 27, a corrections officer with one son. Still, ensemble baths-and-feedings took two hours; the tots ran through 70 disposable diapers a day; and those calling about that "nanny wanted" ad usually didn't pursue the job on hearing they'd have to deal with a full house.

TARO YAMASAKI

Fight fans in Atlantic City for Spinks vs. Tyson also caught a nifty undercard: **SEAN** vs. **MADONNA.** Both were trying to forget their '87 stinker, *Shanghai Surprise*: he, 28, via a play in L.A. and she, 30, by way of party-hopping with comic Sandra Bernhard. The Penns had threatened before to untie their 1985 knots; this time they did.

RON GALELLA

As if to prove that the rumors about his health were just a load of WKRP, **BURT REYNOLDS,** 52, wed **LONI ANDERSON,** 41. (Rather than AIDS, he had suffered two years with temporomandibular joint disorder, caused by a mishap filming 1984's *City Heat.)* It was his second marriage and her third.

MARIO CASILLI / SHOOTING STAR

Having dated Michael Jordan and Eddie Murphy, actress **ROBIN** ***(Head of the Class)*** **GIVENS** took as her husband an even heavierweight: unbeaten champ **MIKE TYSON.** But eight months later, Givens, 24, threw in the towel, saying that Tyson, 22, had used her as a punching bag. Because of her rep for arrogance (she was booed at her own college graduation), Tyson seemed the injured party —until he was jailed in 1992 for the rape of a young beauty contestant.

LORI GRINKER / CONTACT (BOTH)

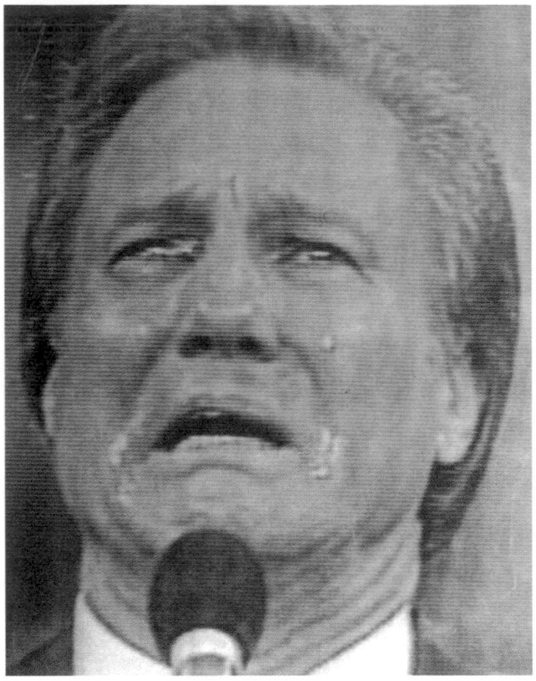

It seemed like the '60s redux: Cries of *¡Huelga!* filled the air and a legion of 90210 liberals, along with **JESSE JACKSON,** were on hand in Delano, California, to mark the end of a 36-day, water-only fast by **CESAR CHAVEZ** (to dramatize a new United Farm Workers concern, the agricultural industry's reliance on pesticides that were potential health threats). Chavez died in 1993, at 66.

JOHN STOREY

In the 24 years since his last good night to Gracie, **GEORGE BURNS** had made a monthly visit to Los Angeles' Forest Lawn Cemetery, where Grace Allen, his comedic partner for 40 years and wife for 38, rests. Now, in *Gracie: A Love Story,* he wryly memorialized her in print: "Gracie married me for laughs, not for sex," wrote Burns, 92. "Of course, she got both of them—when we had sex, she laughed."

HARRY BENSON

Great bawls of fire-and-brimstone! A year earlier, teleminister **JIMMY LEE SWAGGART** (*left*), a high school dropout and cousin to rocker Jerry Lee Lewis, had decried Jim Bakker's carnal ways; now he was repenting his own visits to a New Orleans prostitute (she posed for nude snapshots). Elders of the Assemblies of God, to whom Swaggart, 52, answered (as well as tithed $14 million a year), were Christian about it, lifting his video preacher's license for all of 90 days.

COURTESY OF WBRZ-TV

The house of horrors sat on a genteel, tree-lined block of Manhattan's Greenwich Village. From it, the hideously battered **HEDDA NUSSBAUM,** 45, emerged alive. But the hideously battered Lisa Steinberg, 6, illegally adopted by Hedda and lawyer Joel Steinberg, 46, did not. Nussbaum wasn't charged in exchange for testifying against him and agreeing to institutionalized psychiatric care. Steinberg was nailed for first-degree manslaughter and handed an 8½-to-25-year prison sentence.

DONNA FERRATO / DOMESTIC ABUSE AWARENESS PROJECT

Among the Seoulful delights of the Summer Olympics: Sprinter **FLORENCE GRIFFITH JOYNER,** who proved that the perfect accessory to her racy track suits and lacquered four-inch nails was gold (for the 100- and 200 meter and the 400-meter relay; she also won a silver). At 28, Flo Jo traded her cleats for motherhood and a try at a career as (what else?) a fashion designer.

DIRCK HALSTEAD / GAMMA-LIAISON

U.S. Treasury poster boy **MARK KOSTABI,** 27 (*near right*), presided over a one-off New York City atelier. The native of Whittier, California, paid no-name painters to deliver unsigned canvases (average fee: $100), then added his own autograph and retailed them for as much as $30,000. Patrons knew the works to be mass-produced but cared not; Kostabi called his style "social surrealism" —and they bought it.

PETER SERLING

With psyche intact again after her devastating victimization by John Hinckley Jr. (and frame sleek again after four years of Yale dorm food), **JODIE FOSTER** made a triumphant Hollywood return with three pictures. One—*The Accused*—won the actress, 26, an Oscar for her portrayal of a gang-raped trailer-camp coquette who refuses to remain silent as a lamb.

OUTLINE

REMCO

1989

Like all cartoonists, **MATT GROENING,** 35, had a tough row to ho-hos. But when the family of dysfunctional weak-chins he had drawn as fillers for *The Tracey Ullman Show* proved a laff riot, Fox had him turn them into prime-time's first animated half-hour series since *The Flintstones.* Next season, the fledgling net brashly moved *The Simpson*s (*from left,* **BART, LISA, HOMER, MARGE** and **MAGGIE)** opposite TV's ranking show. Bill Cosby eyed his slumping ratings —and promptly had a cow.

MARK SENNET

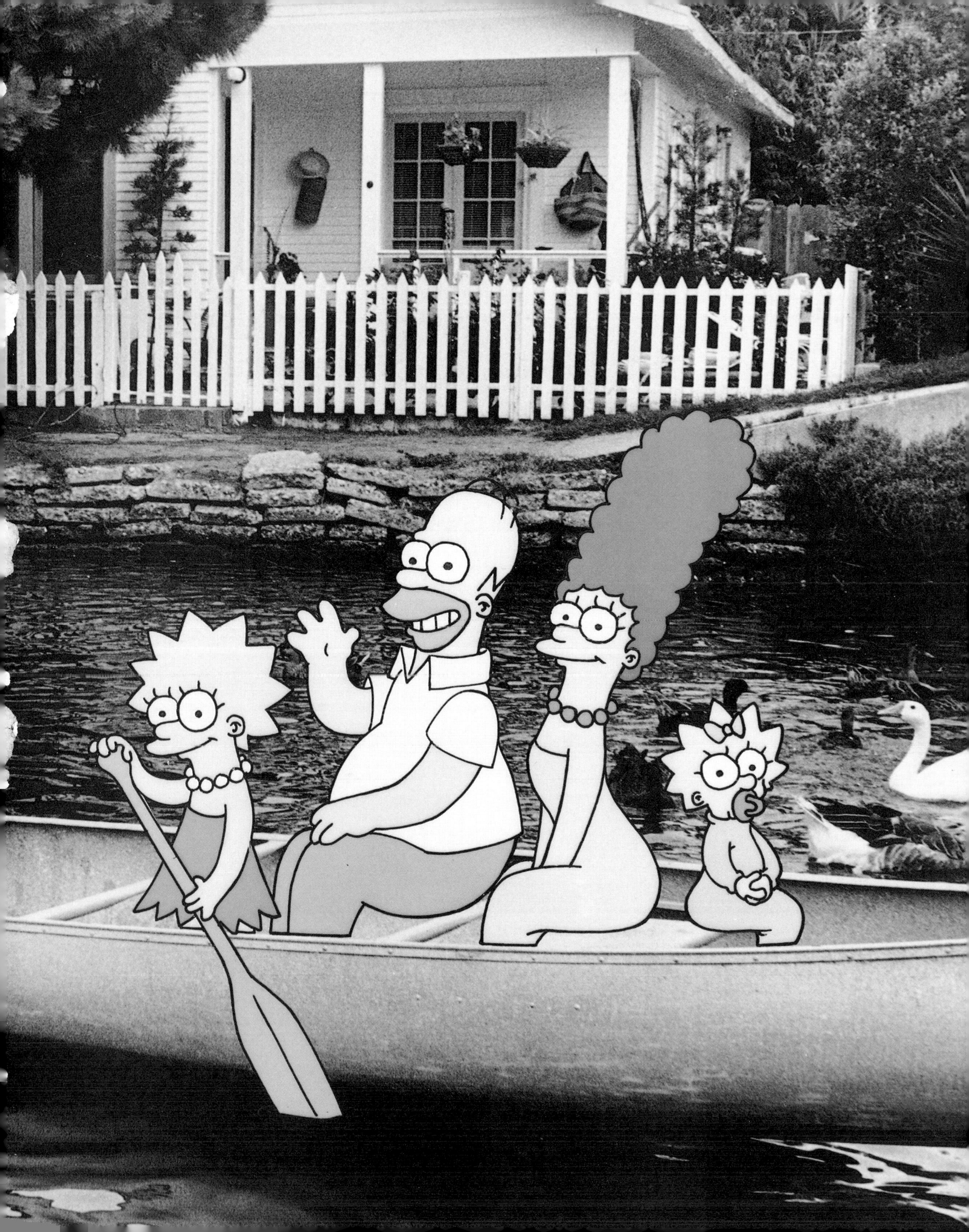

Rust suddenly appears across the breadth of the Iron Curtain. In East Germany, the Berlin Wall tumbles. In Poland, Lech Walesa's Solidarity Party wins a parliamentary majority. In Czechoslovakia, dissident playwright Vaclav Havel, 58, goes from jail to the presidency and Alexander Dubcek, 65, father of 1968's Prague Spring, returns from internal exile to become parliamentary chairman. In Hungary, late despot Janos Kadar's successors repudiate Communism. In Romania, Nicolae Ceausescu, 71, is ousted and, with wife Elena, 73, executed. Fueled by the reforms sweeping Moscow's satellites, citizens in three Soviet republics on the Baltic begin to clamor for freedom. Only Beijing doesn't get it. A student protest against the perks given classmates born to the ruling class escalates into a loud cry for democracy; after a seven-day standoff, senior leader Deng Xiaoping rolls tanks into Tienanmen Square. The toll: 300 dead, 7,000 injured.

Disaster suddenly strikes across the breadth of America. Hurricane Hugo pummels South Carolina. An earthquake clocked at 7.1 on the Richter scale shakes Northern California from Oakland to Watsonville. And the tanker *Exxon Valdez* spills 11 million gallons of crude oil into Alaska's Prince William Sound.

Panama's Manuel Noriega can't win an election, so he brazenly steals it — giving George Bush an excuse to send in U.S. troops. Though the dictator's loyalists are quickly routed, he holes up in the Vatican Embassy for nine days before surrendering. Noriega is flown to Florida where, some two years later, he would be convicted of eight drug-related counts and sentenced to 40 years.

The year's high-techiest fake: "Cold fusion," by which sticking a palladium rod into heavy water is said to generate energy; but Utah scientist Stanley Pons, 50, refuses to share the secret and moves abroad. The year's dumbest fake: Milli Vanilli, whose hit "Girl You Know It's True" was lip-synched; Rob Pilatus, 24, and Fabrice Morvan, 23, must give back their Grammy. The year's funniest fake: Meg Ryan's ham-on-wry orgasm when Harry met Sally to deli-dally.

Passages: Samuel (*Waiting for Godot*) Beckett, 83. Irving Berlin, 101. Mel Blanc, 81 (who gave voice to Bugs, Porky, Daffy & gang). Travel essayist Bruce Chatwin, 49. Salvador Dali, 85. Hirohito, Emperor of Japan, 87 (ending the 63-year Showa Dynasty). Pianist Vladimir Horowitz, 85. Christine Jorgenson, 62 (36 years after her sex-change surgery). Author Mary McCarthy, 77. Laurence Olivier, 82. Boxer Sugar Ray Robinson, 67. Soviet physicist Andrei Sakharov, 68 (winner of the 1975 Nobel Peace Prize for his lonely stand against totalitarian repression). Secretariat, 19. Thomas Sopwith, 101 (designer of the World War I British fighter plane, the Camel, whose pilots would include Snoopy). Hanoi diplomat Le Duc Tho, 79 (whose Vietnam War-ending negotiations with Henry Kissinger won them a joint 1973 Nobel Peace Prize, which Tho declined). Historian Barbara Tuchman, 77. Fashion czarina Diana Vreeland, late-80s.

After taking 48 years to realize that *All I Needed to Know I Learned in Kindergarten,* Robert Fulghum, 52, dishes up more homily grits in *It Was on Fire When I Lay Down on It* and becomes the first to hold both the No.1 and 2 slots on the best-seller list. And debuting on late-night TV, Arsenio Hall, 33, succeeds where Cavett, Griffin, Rivers, Sajak et al. have not: opposite Carson. Woof, woof.

Resembling a modern-day Ripoff van Winkle, Wall Street inside trader IVAN BOESKY, 52, was freed after just 22 months in the pokey (payback for ratting on Michael Milken). Nor did jail make him recant his "Greed is healthy" credo. In 1993, he sued his $100-millionairess ex-wife for alimony and accepted, grudgingly, a $20 million lump-sum payment plus $3,500 a week for life.

PAUL ADAO / NEW YORK POST

It was coming up on two years in jail for D.C. plastic surgeon ELIZABETH MORGAN, 42, who refused to surrender her child by former husband Eric Foretich, 46, an oral surgeon. Hilary had been 5 when Morgan sent her into hiding, claiming Foretich was molesting the girl. In September, Morgan was freed; she later moved to Christchurch, New Zealand, to rejoin her daughter.

EVELYN FLORET

SPIKE

Having directed two low-budget pictures with nary a Caucasian cast member in sight, **SPIKE LEE** sure got Whitey's attention with *Do the Right Thing*. Pundits warned that his corrosive comedy about a Brooklyn ghetto's descent into race warfare would incite real-life violence. It didn't, even though Lee ended the picture with an angry quotation from Malcolm X—whose life he would film in 1992.

MICHAEL ABRAMSON

No tag team this side of "Rowdy" Roddy Piper and The Iron Sheik of Iran boasted more poundage—and *Roseanne* was a lot funnier than pro wrestling. Built around the blue-choleric stand-up act of **ROSEANNE BARR,** 35, and tempered by the teddy-bear huggability of **JOHN GOODMAN,** 36, the show was a throwback to earlier Joe Sixpackcoms like *The Life of Riley* and *The Honeymooners*. It premiered at No. 5 and stayed near the top, not by mocking family values but by redefining them—a lesson some politicians failed to heed in 1992.

TONY COSTA / OUTLINE (BOTH)

MARIANNE WIGGINS of Lancaster, Pennsylvania (*near left*) and Pakistan-born, British-reared **SALMAN RUSHDIE,** both 41, were newlyweds with much to anticipate: publication of hers-and-his novels, *John Dollar* and *The Satanic Verses.* But his book affronted Islamic radicals, so the Ayatollah Khomeini put a bounty on Rushdie's head. Placed under 24-hour guard by the British, he went deep underground. The couple divorced in 1993, the year Iran's rulers said the *fatwa* could be lifted only by Khomeini—who died four months after issuing it.

TERRY SMITH

Seventieth-birthday boy **MALCOLM FORBES** took a buss-man's holiday with **ELIZABETH TAYLOR,** one of 800 pals the magazine publisher jetted to his retreat in Tangiers, Morocco, for a bash that set him back an estimated $2 million. Because Taylor, 57, went Harleying with Forbes and accepted his lavish gifts, there was talk of nuptials. Not until he died in 1991 did his homosexuality become publicly known.

TERRY SMITH

If there is sentient life in the Arcturus Constellation, 36 light-years distant, the TV waves reaching them from Earth were still carrying first-run episodes of *I Love Lucy* when star **LUCILLE BALL,** 77, succumbed to a ruptured aorta. The medium's First Lady of comedy was the last surviving principal (William Frawley having died in 1966, Vivian Vance in 1979 and Ball's ex, **DESI ARNAZ,** in 1986) of an eternally funny show.

NEAL PETERS

Only later was it obvious that **PRINCESS DIANA,** 30, had already entered the dog days of marriage. In covertly-taped phone calls not leaked until 1992 and 1993, Di was heard blowing kisses down the line to chum James Gilbey and Prince Charles lewdly chatting up an old flame, Camilla Parker Bowles.

DAVE CHANCELLOR / ALPHA / GLOBE

Talk about a big year for the First Springer Spaniel: After **MILLIE,** 3, whelped a litter of six (to the joy of **BARBARA BUSH** and First Granddaughter **MARSHALL,** 4), she saw *Millie's Book,* which gave us a sniff of White House life, paw its way to best-sellerdom and fetch more than $800,000 in royalties.

DAVID VALDEZ / THE WHITE HOUSE

Though in the final stages of throat cancer, **SAMMY DAVIS JR.** insisted on gracing a United Negro College Fund-raiser in L.A. —and in turn got a joyous farewell from such friends as Eddie Murphy, Goldie Hawn, Clint Eastwood, **LOLA FALANA** (*far left*), **JESSE JACKSON, MICHAEL JACKSON, ELLA FITZGERALD** and **QUINCY JONES.** Six months later, Davis was dead at the age of 64.

LAURA D. LUONGO / PETER BORSARI

On trial for embezzling $158 million from his PTL empire, unplugged TV minister **JIM BAKKER,** 49, tried tears and even public anxiety attacks as a defense. No sale: The jury said guilty and the judge said 18 years. He even lost Tammy Faye, who was rewed to onetime Bakker pal Roe Messner in a 1993 ceremony sold to TV's *A Current Affair* for $75,000.

CHUCK BURTON / ASSOCIATED PRESS

PETE ROSE, 48, had to hang up his glove when baseball commissioner Bart Giamatti came down with a hardball decree. For placing wagers on major-league games, the player-manager with gilt-edged Cooperstown credentials (a most-ever 3,562 games played; a most-ever 4,256 base hits; three World Series rings; 17 All-Star appearances) was banned for life and ruled ineligible to enter the Hall of Fame.

MICHAEL A. SMITH

The 1960s, in which ABC's sleeper hit, *The Wonder Years,* was set, came to an end seven years before its star, **FRED SAVAGE,** was born. No matter; the series shied away from sit-ins and love-ins and acid rock to focus on one boy's passage through puberty. Fred himself was starting to think about girls, mostly a daughter of family friends who was nice and funny and, best of all, could burp on cue.
HARRY BENSON

Where's the rest of me hair? Shaved off, actually, by a pre-op team before **RONALD REAGAN,** 78, underwent surgery to remove fluid on the brain (a condition that dated back to a riding spill suffered on a post-White House vacation in Mexico). Meanwhile, **NANCY,** 68, was either contemplating giving up astrology for phrenology or merely playing veil to the chief.
JIM MONE / ASSOCIATED PRESS

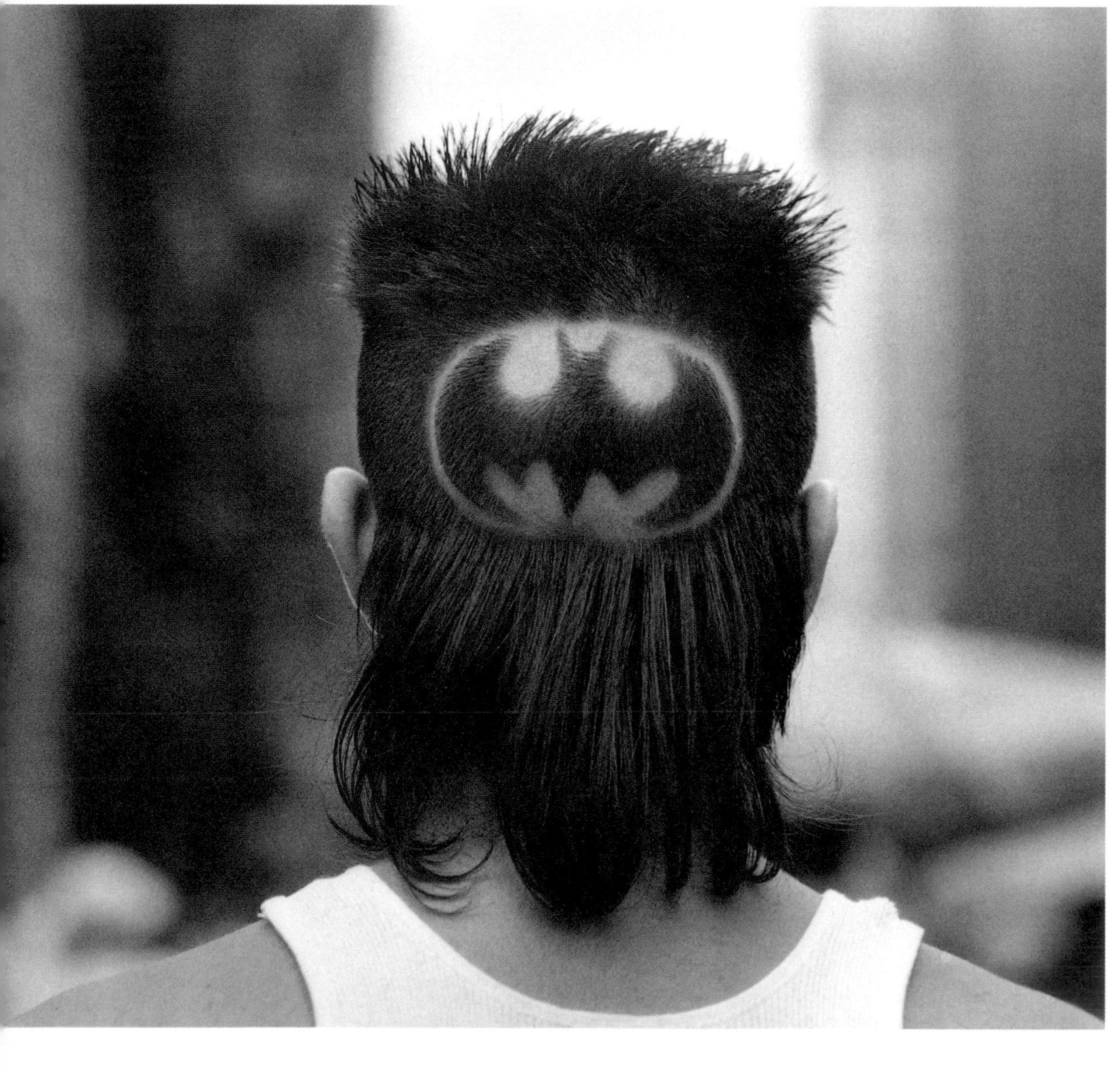

Was the summer's biggest multiplex-filler a trifle overmerchandised? Even hair stylists snared a cut of **BATMANIA,** with prices at trendier New York City chop shops starting at $35. No doubt their belfry-challenged clients would then roar off in a taxi, also known as the bat-out-of-hellmobile.
ANDY LEVIN

The Arctic blast causing **WILLARD SCOTT**'s carpet to fly came not from Canada but from *Today* colleague Bryant Gumble, who wrote an eyes-only memo that was fed to a tabloid. In it, Gumble, 40, scathingly critiqued the show and found its $1-million-a-year weatherman, 55, overpaid and unfunny ("This guy is killing us"). Scott, who never met a 100-year-old he didn't like, joked that he might "have a mob of centenarians find Bryant and gum him to death."
CHRISTOPHER LITTLE

1990

Gone was the last of the baby chub swaddling her in 1988's *Mystic Pizza* and *Satisfaction;* gone too was the adolescent gawkiness of her doomed Dixie belle in 1989's *Steel Magnolias.* At 23, **JULIA ROBERTS** had bloomed into a ravishing (and endearing) *Pretty Woman* —and a Hollywood star of the first magnitude.

E.J. CAMP / OUTLINE

Free Nelson Mandela!, read posters around the world. Incoming South African president F. W. de Klerk, 53, does just that. Then he and the African National Congress leader, who has spent nearly 28 of his 71 years in confinement, begin the negotiations to dismantle apartheid that would in 1993 win them a joint Nobel Peace Prize. Cowabunga!, declaim the Teenage Mutant Ninja Turtles. No dude is Violeta Barrios de Chamorro, but she achieves what the back half of Iran-contra could not: unseat Nicaragua's Sandinistas. Aided by a rapidly deteriorating economy, the 60-year-old newspaper publisher outpolls Daniel Ortega, 44, who relinquishes the presidency (but not all power; his supporters retain key government posts).

Remember Pearl Harbor!, gripe xenophobes. Japan may own 28 percent of the U.S. new-car market, as well as all-American symbols ranging from Rockefeller Center to Pebble Beach Golf Course, but does let one treasure get away. He is first baseman Cecil Fielder, 32, who after fattening up on Japanese pitching for a season comes home to club 51 homers for the Detroit Tigers.

Heavenly embarassment of riches: the $1.5-billion Hubble telescope, which is as big as a bus but as myopic as Mr. Magoo (because its lenses were faultily ground). Earthly embarassment of riches: Brian de Palma's long-awaited $40 million *Bonfire of the Vanities* (forget *Heaven's Gate* as a synonym for failure).

When Daisy Wilson Cave, who is between 97 and 105, dies in Sumter, South Carolina, newspapers call her the last Confederate widow. "I'm still here," rebuts Alberta Martin, 83, of Alba, Alabama. In December, 1927, at age 21, she wed William Jasper Martin, then in his late 70s, who served in the Civil War with the 4th Alabama Infantry. In Michigan, retired pathologist Jack Kervorkian, 62, responds to the pleas of an Alzheimer's sufferer by assisting Janet Adkins, 54, of Portland, Oregon, to end her life; he soon hears from the Wayne County prosecutor, as well as others suffering debilitating or terminal illnesses.

Passages: Harry Angstrom, 60-ish (killed off by novelist John Updike after almost 30 years and four "Rabbit" novels). Pearl Bailey, 72. Leonard Bernstein, 72. Psychologist Bruno (*The Uses of Enchantment*) Bettelheim, 86. Composer Aaron Copland, 90. Former Clearance Creedwater Revivalist Tom Fogerty, 48. Greta Garbo, 84. Ava Gardner, 67. Satirist Ray (of Bob and Ray) Goulding, 68. Status-luggagemaker Aldo Gucci, 84. Cat cartoonist B. Kliban, 55. Mary Martin, 76. CBS founder William Paley, 89. Barbara Stanwyck, 82. Rodeo champ Casey Tibbs, 60. Novelist and listmaker Irving Wallace, 74.

The Rumalia oil field, one of the world's largest known reserve, lies beneath both Iraq and Kuwait, an inconvenient fact that has been the source of past squabbles. Now, Saddam Hussein again complains that the neighboring kingdom is extracting more than its fair share of crude and, to demonstrate his resolve, mobilizes for war. Eight days after being assured by the U.S. Ambassador to Iraq that America would not involve itself in a faraway border dispute, he green-lights the Iraqi army, which needs but 12 hours to conquer Kuwait. Five days later, the first American ground troops hit the Persian Gulf. Near year's end, as more nations sign on to Operation Desert Shield and dispatch forces, Hussein vows that the looming conflict will be the Mother of All Battles.

DAVID LYNCH, 44, transferred the off-kilter vision that had informed movies like *Eraserhead* and *Blue Velvet* to TV via a whodunit as feverish as its Pacific Northwest characters: Leo the Human Cauliflower, the Log Lady, even a dancing dwarf. But despite a cult following and two Emmys, *Twin Peaks* proved to be, like the late Laura Palmer, too much the tease; ABC was forced to play serial killer after only 30 episodes.

DAVID STRICK / ONYX

Two days after Saddam Hussein sent Iraqi tanks into Kuwait, America's top grunt, **COLIN POWELL,** finished mapping a rapid-deployment response. The youngest officer and first black to chair the Joint Chiefs of Staff, Powell, a much decorated Vietnam veteran, then oversaw the retooling of Desert Shield into Desert Storm. In 1993, at 56, he stepped down from his $131,368-a-year post and accepted an advance of $6.5 million to write his memoirs.

ROBERT TRIPPETT / SIPA PRESS

The California Highway Patrol could protect visitor **DAN QUAYLE** from harm but not from zingers (Hear they're making a movie about his Vietnam experiences? It's called *Full Dinner Jacket).* The Veep, 43, didn't help himself with his gift for gaffes; trying at a United Negro College Fund luncheon to invoke the group's slogan (A Mind Is a Terrible Thing to Waste), he blurted, "What a waste it is to lose one's mind."

MARK SENNET / ONYX

Jack-of-all-music **QUINCY JONES** had only to look in the mirror to see his own mortality: The forehead scar left by surgeons who saved him from two near-fatal brain aneurysms in 1974. Having trumpeted with Basie, Hampton, Bird and Dizzy before turning to scoring movies (*Cactus Flower, The Color Purple)* and producing pop hits (for singers from Lesley Gore to Michael Jackson), Jones, 57, was now a fresh prince of Bel-Air (the title also of his company's new sitcom).

HARRY BENSON

In prime time, **DANA DELANEY** *(left)* changed into fatigues and scrubs to patrol another stretch of sand: *China Beach*. The Vietnam series, set at an in-country Army hospital, was played as drama, not comedy, and Delaney's war-zone-toughened nurse was hardly a hot-lipped Houlihan. All of which didn't stop mail call from bringing the Emmy winner, 34, bagfuls of mash notes.

HARRY BENSON

His Sophie had faced just such a choice: In 1985, **WILLIAM STYRON** had considered taking his own life. Unlike his heroine, he didn't. Instead of walking in front of an oncoming truck, the novelist heeded his family and friends and consulted a psychiatrist. Diagnosed as clinically depressed, weaned from Halcion (prescribed earlier for his insomnia) and briefly hospitalized, Styron recovered and at 65 recounted his ordeal in *Darkness Visible: A Memoir of Madness*, his first nonfiction best-seller.

JOHN LOENGARD

Miami Rebound Machine: Just three months earlier, 32-year-old **GLORIA ESTEFAN**'s spine had been mangled when her tour bus was rear-ended by a semi on a highway in Pennsylvania and hurled into the back of a stalled truck. (The accident also broke the collarbone of her son Nayib, 9, but left husband **EMILIO,** 37, unscathed.) Yet a year after the crash, Estefan—two steel rods implanted in her lower back—was again *Conga*-ing on stage.

HARRY BENSON

America was rolling again, thanks to Minneapolis's Scott and Brennan Olson. Their summer trainer for hockey players also won over aerobics buffs, who liked the low-impact **IN-LINE SKATES** (if not the $100-and-up prices).

TONY COSTA / OUTLINE

At 44, **GOLDIE HAWN**'s Airhead Jordan shtick may have been losing its point (the disappointing grosses for 1987's *Overboard* and her new *Bird on a Wire* were no laugh-in matter). But her seven-year, one-child relationship with Kurt Russell, 39, stayed above the rim. And at least Disney thought she had box-office legs; the studio signed Hawn to a seven-picture, $30 million pact.

TONY COSTA / OUTLINE

If James Brown was the hardest-working man In showbiz, what was **M.C. HAMMER**—chopped collard greens? The 27-year-old rapper from Oakland (né Stanley Kirk Burrell) with the faster-than-Michael feet and the billowing harem pants sold a year's-best 8 million albums and played 250 live dates. The title of his megasingle about nailed it: "U Can't Touch This."

CO RENTMEESTER

It went without saying that **MADONNA** put up a good front on her latest tour. The busy singer, 31, also had a modest role in *Dick Tracy* and a more prominent one in the life of the movie's producer-director-star, Warren Beatty, 53 (at least until, as filmed by the makers of her 1991 *Truth or Dare* rockumentary, she took to dissing him backstage at a Blond Ambition concert).

NEAL PRESTON

Sure, the guy could give good baseball (*Bull Durham, Field of Dreams*). But now he was plotting a three-hour-plus Western in which a cavalryman goes native American? With the Indians speaking authentic dialects? And he wanted to direct too? Yup, **KEVIN COSTNER**, 35, did almost everything but sire a Sioux named Boy—and *Dances with Wolves* waltzed off with seven Oscars and a gross of $184 million.

JONATHAN EXLEY / GAMMA-LIAISON

Fourteen years after his classic three-volume *The Civil War: A Narrative* was published, **SHELBY FOOTE** went back to the sites, from Fort Sumter to Appomattox, as host of an 11-hour documentary by Ken Burns that was PBS's highest-rated series ever. Of achieving media fame at age 73, the historian-novelist declared, "I'm looking forward to when my 15 minutes are over."

JOHN LOENGARD

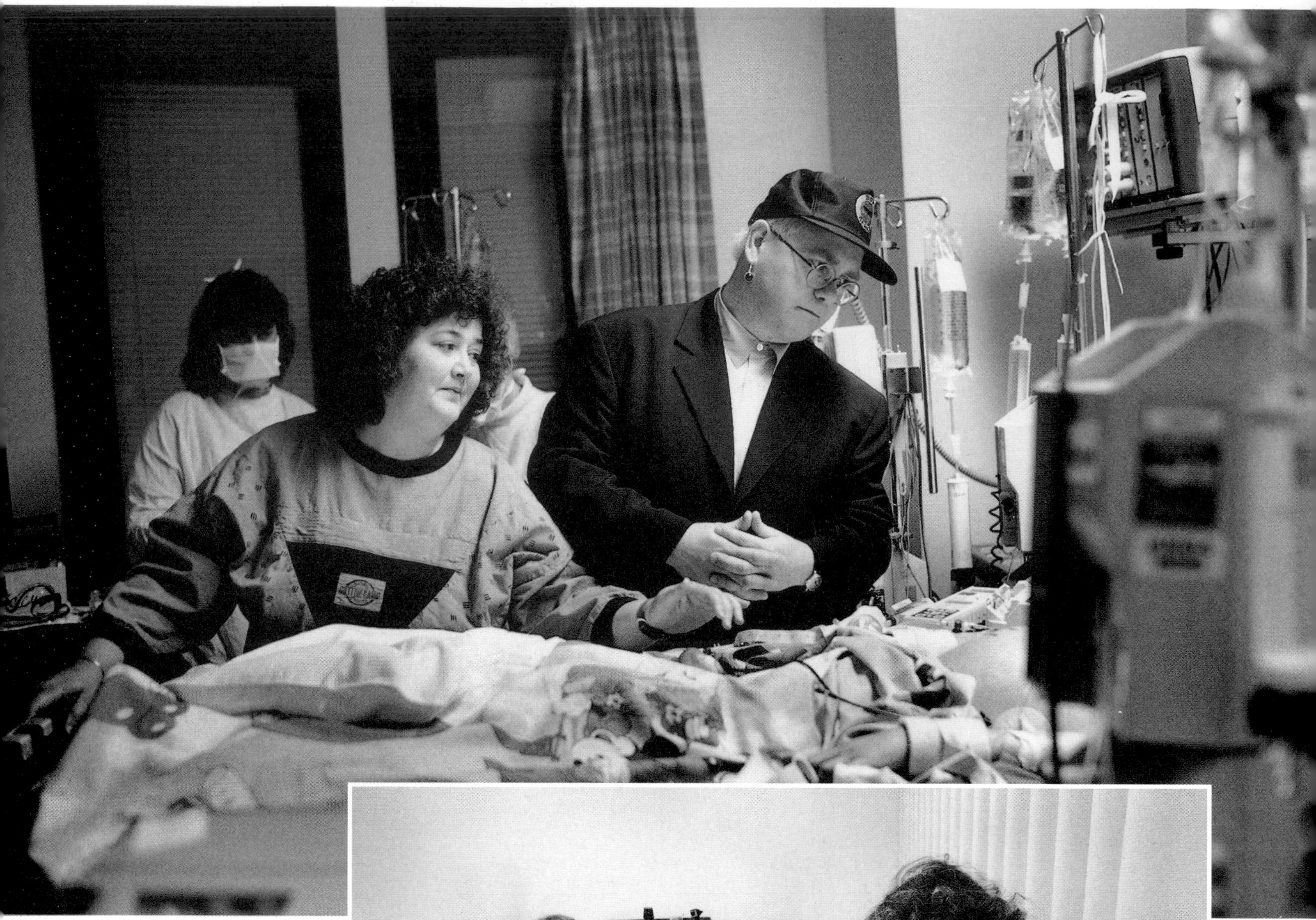

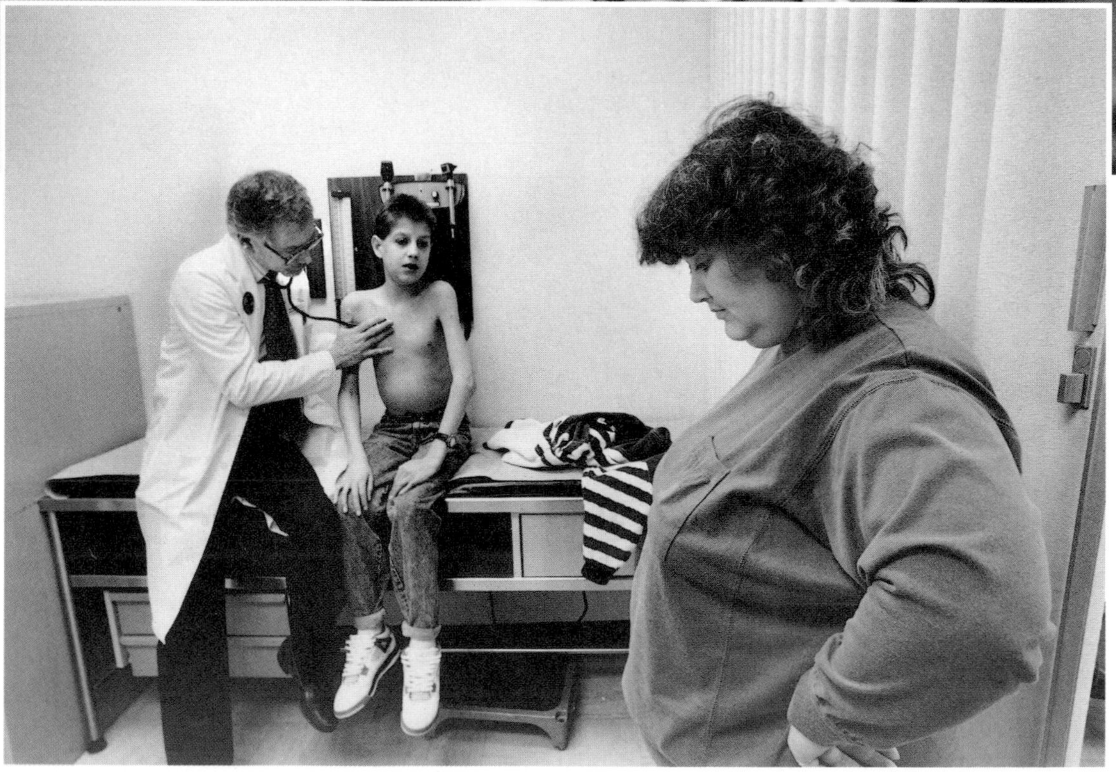

For six years, **RYAN WHITE** fought off death and, almost as painful, an ignorance-fueled hysteria over the AIDS that was killing him. A hemophiliac transfused with tainted blood, Ryan and Mom **JEANNE** had to sue the Kokomo, Indiana, schools to keep him in class. Near the end, **ELTON JOHN,** an early and unwavering family supporter, joined the Whites. Hours after John crashed a nearby Farm Aid Concert to sing "Candle in the Wind" for his young friend, Ryan's fight ended. He was 18.

TARO YAMASAKI (BOTH)

From his hat he had pulled fresh icons for childhood in the electronic age: the Muppets and Big Bird too, plus pay-cable's Fraggle Rockers and movies from the Miss Piggy musicals to fantasies like *Dark Crystal* and *Labyrinth*. With an empire to guide, **JIM HENSON** ignored an onset of fatigue and sniffles. Had he sought prompt care, his rare staph infection could have been treated. Instead, just three days later, Henson was dead at the age of 53.

HENSON ASSOCIATES

PRINCESS CAROLINE, 33, was in Paris when she learned the news: Down in Monaco, husband No. 2, Stefano Casiraghi, 30, had died after flipping his craft in a powerboat race (a sport he had vowed to quit). In 1992, the Vatican granted her long-standing petition to annul marriage No. 1, and later declared Caroline's three children by Casiraghi to be indeed legitimate.

KEN GOFF

1991

Despite Saddam Hussein's taunts, **NORMAN SCHWARZKOPF** was a paper tiger only to wife **BRENDA,** 50, and son **CHRISTIAN,** 13 (who hammed it up with a life-size cutout at Gulf War's end). Desert-Stormin' Norman, 56 (*below*), left home for 239 days to lead 700,000 American and allied troops in the rout of Iraq, then left the Army after 35 years to pen his best-selling 1992 memoirs, *It Doesn't Take a Hero*.

HARRY BENSON (BOTH)

U.S. ARMY

Softened up by 43 days of bombardment from 126,000 Western coalition aerial sorties and warship-launched Tomahawk cruise missiles, Saddam Hussein's vaunted military machine receives the Mother of All Drubbings. Only later, when the unrepentant Hussein takes out his frustrations by slaughtering Kurdish secessionists in Iraq's north and Muslim insurgents in the south, would questions arise about who called off Desert Storm after 100 hours, and why. In a war fought largely out of news-camera range, the stocks of two telejournalists soar: CNN's Peter Arnett, 56, for his reports from the Al Rasheed Hotel in the heart of besieged Baghdad, and NBC's Arthur Kent, 37, for his play-by-plays of the Iraqi Scud missiles falling near his base of operation in Dhahran, Saudi Arabia. ("The Satellite Dish," as he is dubbed by some female admirers, would quit the network in 1992 owing to unhappiness with his post-Gulf assignments).

The new world order proves short-lived. Civil war erupts in Yugoslavia as Croatia and Slovenia secede. And Sergei Krikalev, 33, becomes a poignant metaphor for the events that rock the Soviet Union. On May 18, the Cosmonaut Third Class is shuttled up to begin a five-month tour aboard the space station Mir — whose 16 orbits per day soon seem slow compared with events on the ground. In August, Mikhail Gorbachev, 60, is imprisoned at his Black Sea dacha by coupsters. His surprise rescuer: old foe Boris Yeltsin, 60. Four months later, Yeltsin succeeds Gorbachev as the head of a state that he then dissolves. Because of political instability and budgetary problems, Krikalev is left aloft. He would eventually land, after 313 days, in not the USSR but in the C.I.S. (Commonwealth of Independent States), and find that even his hometown of Leningrad has been renamed, to St. Petersburg.

Chicago, though, stays Chicago, where Macauley Culkin also remains when left *Home Alone.* At least his mom isn't Wanda Holloway, 37, of Midchannel, Texas; when her 14-year-old daughter does not make the cheerleading squad, Holloway puts out a contract on the mother of a girl who did. (The hitman, however, turns out to be a police informer whose testimony would help earn Holloway a 15-year term in prison).

Passages: Actress Jean Arthur, 90. Physicist John Bardeen, 82 (a double Nobel Prizewinner, including in 1956 for coinventing the transistor). Miles Davis, 65. Travel guidester Eugene Fodor, 85. Prima ballerina Margot Fonteyn, 71. Redd Foxx, 68. Theodore Geisel, 87 (who as Dr. Seuss wrote *The Cat in the Hat* and other rhyme-happy fables). Contract bridge authority Charles Goren, 90. Rock impresario Bill Graham, 60. Modern-dance mistress Martha Graham, 96. Ski and tennis equipmentmaker Howard Head, 75. Automaker Sochiro Honda, 84. Edwin Land, 81 (inventor of the Polaroid camera). Moviemaker David Lean, 83. Yves Montand, 70. *Star Trek* creator Gene Roddenberry, 70.

Late one night in North Hollywood, California, George Holliday, 31, the manager of a plumbing store, hears a disturbance outside. Grabbing a camcorder, he steps out onto his balcony and begins to tape a cluster of police officers using clubs, boots and fists to quiet a traffic violator. When Holliday offers his footage to a local TV station, Rodney King, 25, is no longer anonymous.

Frankly, my dear, critics didn't give a damn for the novel by ALEXANDRIA RIPLEY, 57. Yet no one save Margaret Mitchell could have sequelized *Gone With the Wind* without censure, and she died in 1949. Mitchell's estate, with the copyright expiring in 2011, hired Ripley to write the critic-proof *Scarlett,* which sold some 2.3 million copies.

HARRY BENSON

Faithfully adhering to Postal Service regs, Fox TV used the zip (*90210*) plus four (*from left,* LUKE PERRY, 26; SHANNEN DOHERTY, 20; JASON PRIESTLY, 22; JENNY GARTH, 19) to make Beverly Hills CA the place for teens in the know(s).

MARK SENNET / ONYX

ANITA HILL had not wanted to appear before the Senate committee examining the fitness of one of her ex-bosses to sit on the Supreme Court. But once subpoenaed, the 35-year-old University of Oklahoma law professor unleashed a tragicomic episode of she-said-he-said by detailing his alleged sexual harassment of her a decade earlier. Nominee **CLARENCE THOMAS,** 43 (with second wife **VIRGINIA,** 34, *below)* responded with a blanket denial and called himself the victim of "a lynch mob." The all-male, all-white Senate panel chose to believe Thomas. A 1993 poll showed most Americans had come to believe Hill.

RICK REINHARD / IMPACT VISUALS (LEFT); HARRY BENSON

The **DORRS** of Bright, Indiana—**GRETI,** 37, a hospital coordinator and **RICK,** 33, an oil company service technician—first saw their new daughter **ADRIANA** in PEOPLE. A picture of the 3-year-old, who suffered congenital deformities, had run with a story on the wretched Romanian orphanages maintained by the ousted Communists. The Dorrs, already the parents of two, spent six months locating and adopting the girl. Once back in America, plucky Adriana endured surgery to correct a club foot and to unfuse three fingers on her left hand, and received a prothesis for her right hand, which she soon mastered.

TARO YAMASAKI

TERRY ANDERSON was kidnapped in Beirut by Muslim extremists just as Ronald Reagan began his second term, *Challenger* was still intact and the newsman's second daughter not yet born. Freed after 2,455 days, Anderson, 44, finally got to see Sulome, 6, who was in attendance when he married her mother, Madeleine Bassil, in 1993.

LUC NOVOVITCH / GAMMA-LIAISON

The Party was over—the Communist Party, that is. Two years after knocking down the infamous Wall that had divided their city for a generation, Berliners got around to remodeling one of the main squares in the old Eastern sector. First to be consigned to the dustbin of history: a 60-foot-high statue, hewn from red granite, of Soviet Founding Father **VLADIMIR I. LENIN.**

HANSKI KRAUSS / ASSOCIATED PRESS

The preconcert ritual—**NAOMI JUDD** touching up her gloss, daughter **WYNONNA** checking her hair—had begun in 1983. But after 18 country chart-toppers, it was time for the duo's farewell tour: Naomi, 45, had incurable chronic active hepatitis, an enervating and sometimes fatal liver disease. Her showbiz legacy included not only Wynonna, at 27 poised to go solo, but also daughter Ashley, 24, who had just won a role on the new NBC series, *Sisters.*

CHRISTOPHER LITTLE

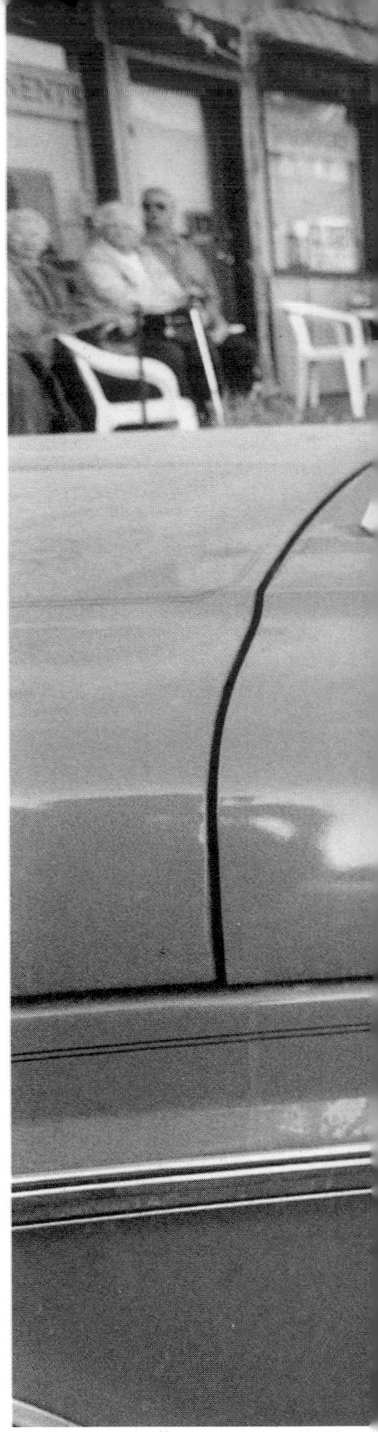

ELIZABETH TAYLOR HILTON WILDING TODD FISHER BURTON BURTON WARNER, 59, met her new fiancée three years earlier at the Betty Ford Clinic, where both were in drug rehab. In October, she and **LARRY FORTENSKY,** 39, who had been a truck driver and construction worker, were wed at the 2,900-acre Santa Barbara, California, estate of her friend Michael Jackson.

DAVID McGOUGH / DMI

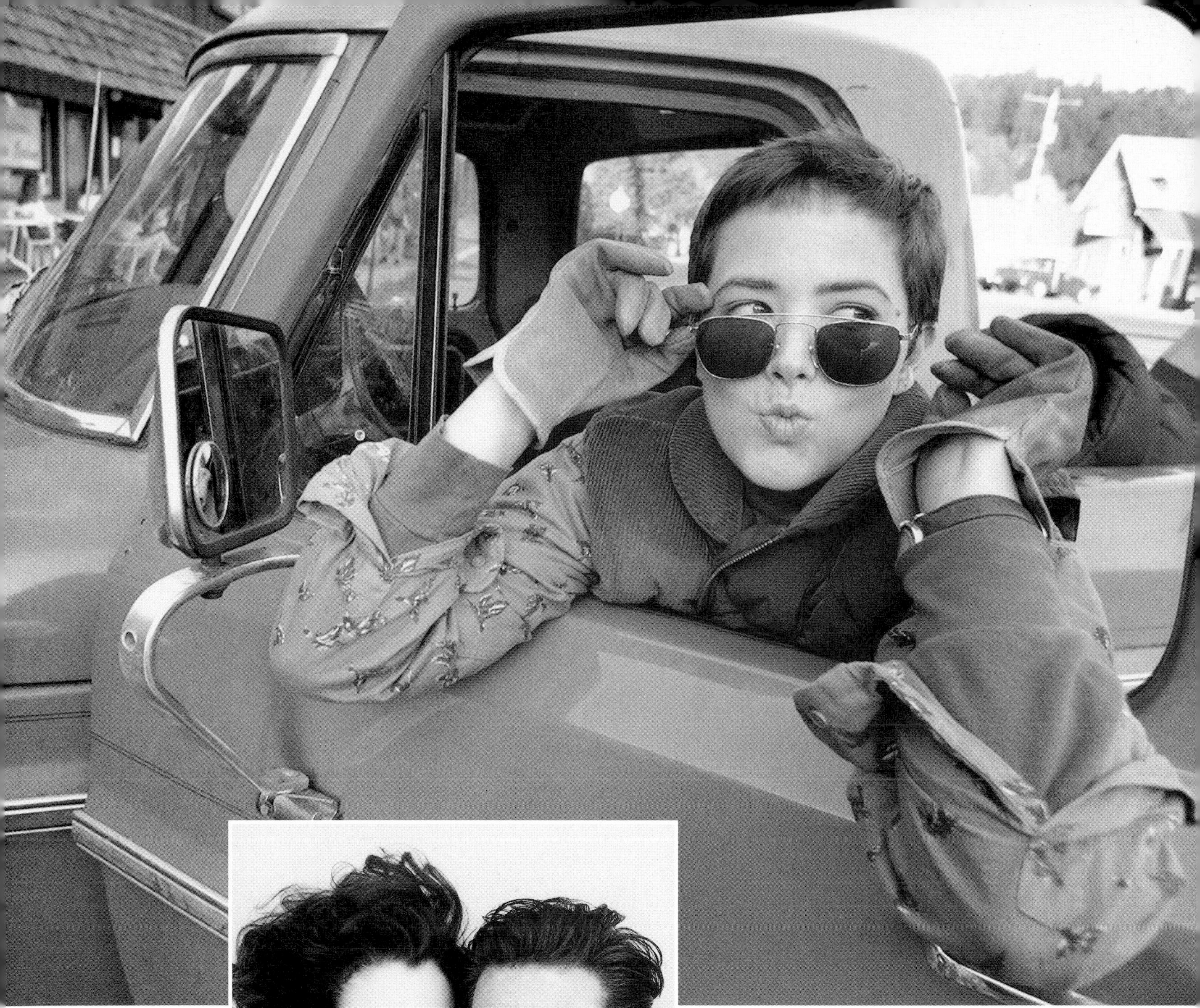

It took him most of a lifetime, but **WARREN BEATTY,** 54, rid himself of the heartbreak of satyriasis when he and *Bugsy* costar **ANNETTE BENING,** 33, revealed she was bearing his child. (To protect her pregnancy, Bening ceded Catwoman's jumpsuit to Michelle Pfeiffer.) The couple wed two months after the birth of Kathlyn Beatty.

PATRICK DEMARCHELIER

JANINE TURNER's puckers sent the men of Cicely, Alaska, running—the other way. On the CBS whimsitcom *Northern Exposure,* she was a bush pilot whose beaus died weird (one was standing under a falling satellite). A soap graduate once best known as a former Alex Baldwin fiancée, Turner, 28, rode her kiss-of-the-glider-woman fame into movies (*Cliffhanger)* and major ads (Chevrolet).

TONY COSTA / OUTLINE

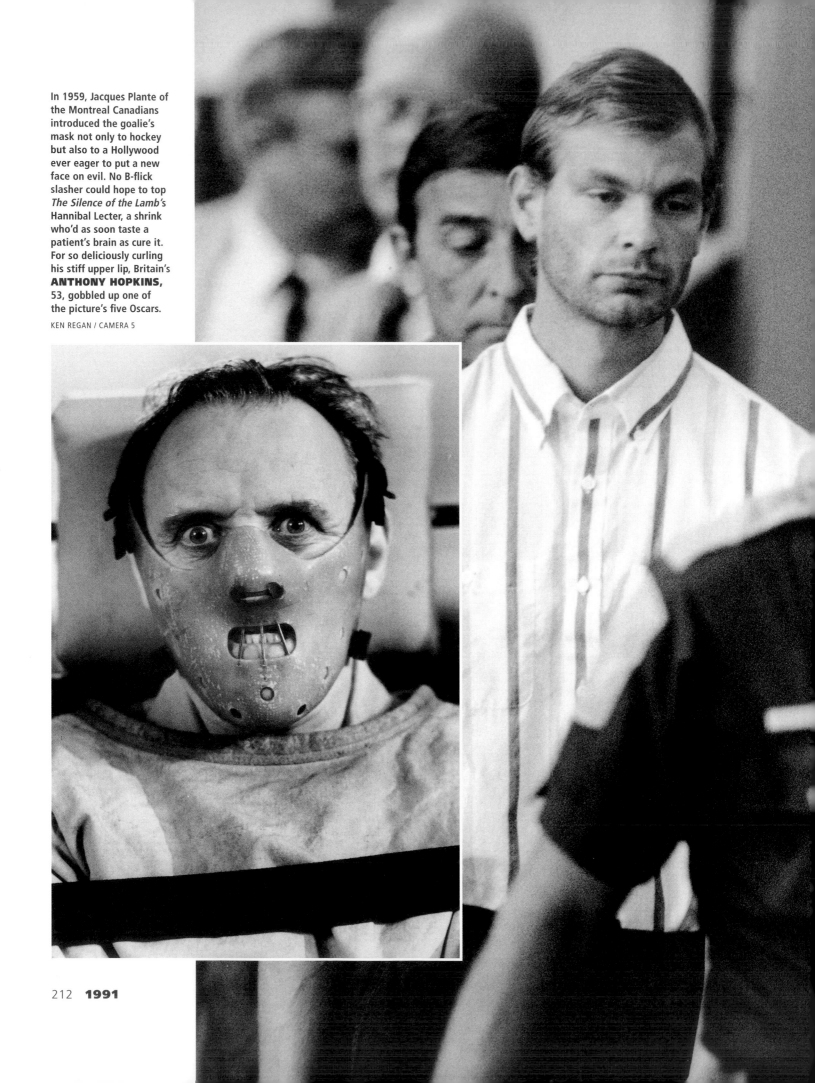

In 1959, Jacques Plante of the Montreal Canadians introduced the goalie's mask not only to hockey but also to a Hollywood ever eager to put a new face on evil. No B-flick slasher could hope to top *The Silence of the Lamb's* Hannibal Lecter, a shrink who'd as soon taste a patient's brain as cure it. For so deliciously curling his stiff upper lip, Britain's **ANTHONY HOPKINS,** 53, gobbled up one of the picture's five Oscars.

KEN REGAN / CAMERA 5

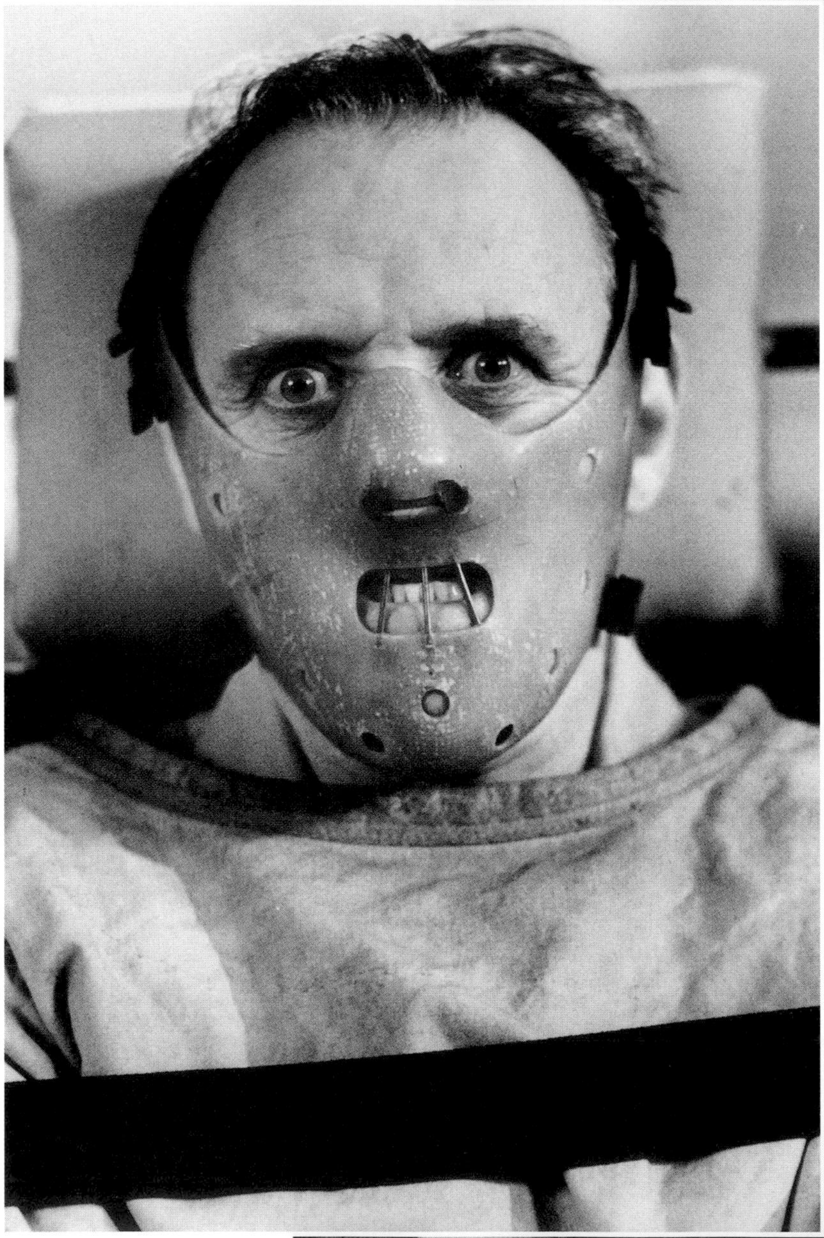

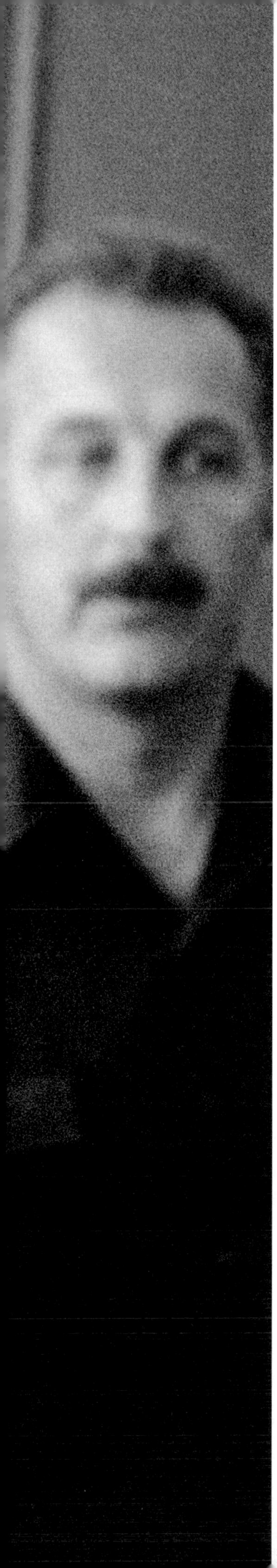

By junior high, he was slaying small mammals and saving their skulls. In high school he murdered his first human. Now 32, he worked in a Milwaukee chocolate factory by day and cruised gay bars by night in search of fresh prey. When caught by police, he admitted killing 17 men whose corpses he would variously violate or dismember or snack on. **JEFFREY DAHMER,** given 15 consecutive life terms, will be eligible for parole in the year 2927.

MORRY GASH / ASSOCIATED PRESS

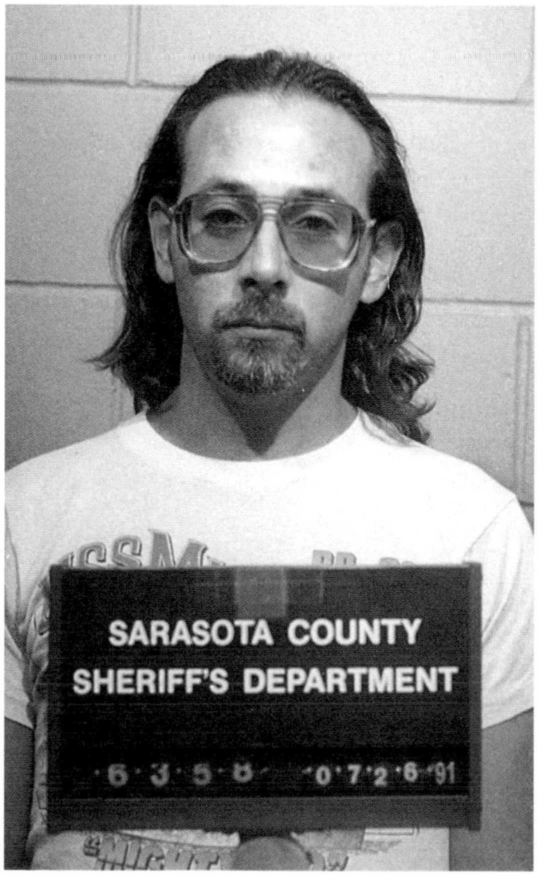

Thelma and Louise was not—repeat, not—the year's primo date movie. **SUSAN SARANDON,** 44 (*left;* she was Louise) and **GEENA DAVIS,** 34, played girls who just want to have fun, only not with the testosteroned crazies along life's highway. Some saw them as feminist martyrs, others as gun-toting bimbos; but to the studio, they were the sequel that can never be.

MGM

They all snickered when **PAUL REUBENS,** the bug-eyed naif Pee-wee Herman of movies and TV, was caught masturbating at an XXX-rated Florida theater (*left).* The actor, 39, turned the tables six weeks later when he opened an MTV awards show by asking, "Heard any good jokes lately?"

GLOBE

When *Billboard* revamped the way it measured CD and tape sales, the pop chart took on a new, big-hatted look: **GARTH BROOKS'**s LP, *Ropin' the Wind,* debuted at No. 1. Once an Oklahoma State javelinist with Olympic hopes, Brooks, 29, settled for collecting gold records that proved Nashville was no one's country cousin.

FRANK MICELOTTA

They may have been Ozzie and Harriet's grandsons, but to the **NELSONS—GUNNAR** *(near right)* and **MATTHEW**—life was no sitcom; folks Rick and Kris Nelson had split when the identical twins were 13. A decade later, the Nelsons had followed their late dad (killed in a 1985 plane crash) into music and onto the pop charts, with "Love and Affection" reaching No. 1.

HARRY BENSON

It wasn't his outlaw image that sicced the revenuers on **WILLIE NELSON** but rather some disallowed tax shelters taken in the '70s. The singer, 57 (with son **LUCAS,** 2), didn't have the $16.7 million in back taxes and penalties, so the IRS seized all assets save his gold records. But when his family ranch was put on the block, the folks whom Nelson had Farm Aided repaid the favor by refusing to bid. In 1993, the Feds settled for $9 million, of which Nelson still owed $5.4 million.

MARK PERLSTEIN

1992

CHELSEA CLINTON had been raised mostly in public housing (the Governor's Mansion in Little Rock). In quest of finer digs, the 12-year-old's parents, **BILL** and **HILLARY RODHAM,** both 45, spent most of the year as Arkansas travelers. It paid off. Overcoming a womanizing reputation that also afflicted his political idol, JFK, Clinton was able on November 3 to tell his daughter that early in the new year, vans would be moving the family's belongings to a grand new address: 1600 Pennsylvania Avenue.

HARRY BENSON

Every general election since 1976 has been such a blowout that even Wayne Campbell and Garth Algar of Aurora, Illinois (and *Wayne's World*), should be able to handicap 1992. With George Bush fresh off the most triumphant year of any recent presidency — Desert Storm; the implosion of the Soviet Union, with its accompanying promise of the long-anticipated "peace dividend"; a field of low-profile Democratic primary contenders — it appears that November 3 will be another laugher . . . *Not!* For as 1988 Democratic Vice Presidential candidate Lloyd Bentsen says, on hearing the results of his party's Connecticut primary, "If Jerry Brown is the answer, it must be a damned peculiar question."

The unalloyed triumphs of the year are simple to tally: speed skater Bonnie Blair and ice skater Kristi Yamaguchi at the Albertville Winter Games; Gail Devers, Carl Lewis, Jackie Joyner-Kersee, Matt Biondi, Nicole Haislett, Dan & Dave (*Not!*) and the Dream Team at the Barcelona Summer Games; Clint Eastwood's *Unforgiven* for adults and Disney's *Aladdin* for kids of all ages.

The disasters take more time to grasp. Hurricane Andrew, which razes large tracts of South Florida, is an act of God. But the record $4.45 billion loss posted by General Motors isn't. Nor is the wrath unleashed by the Rodney King verdict; incinerated are the very parts of Los Angeles that can least afford to rebuild. Some achy breaky heartaches come in smaller packages. Neither Anita Hill nor Clarence Thomas would soon heal from their very public, and very different remembrances of things past. Sadder still is the lawsuit successfully brought by Gregory K., 12, of Orlando, Florida, to divorce his biological mother.

Luckily, there is always politics for comic relief. George Bush is not allowed to forget his stomach woes at a January banquet in Tokyo. Indeed, Dana Carvey, *Wayne's* hurl-happy Garth, performs a parody on *Saturday Night Live* that is in extremely, er, poor taste. That's before Carvey discovers an even riper target; the moment he opens an *SNL* by impersonating a jug-eared Texan waving a personal check for $712 million ("Everything's covered. What I'm saying is that South Central L.A. . . . Problem solved"), Ross Perot is no longer a candidate-come-lately. Meanwhile, Bill Clinton draws the line at inhaling and Dan Quayle, on a visit to a Bronx classroom, turns "potato" into a spelling beee.

Passages: Country singer Roy Acuff, 89. Science fact- and fictionalist Isaac Asimov, 72. Former Israeli Prime Minister Menachem Begin, 78. Marlene Dietrich, 90. Czechoslovakian leader Alexander Dubcek, 70. Nobel Prizewinning geneticist Barbara McClintock, 90. Christian Nelson, 98 (inventor in 1921 of the Eskimo Pie). Longtime Miss America emcee Bert Parks, 77. Moviemaker Satyajit Ray, 70. Cartoonist Joe Shuster, 78 (who in 1934 cocreated *Superman*). Watergate judge John Sirica, 88. Billionaire retailer Sam Walton, 74. Musicmaker Lawrence Welk, 89. Onetime Supreme Mary ("My Guy") Wells, 49.

Finally, bipartisan couple Mary Matalin, 39, and James Carville, 48, must put their relationship on hold: she spins Bush's messages, he plays *consigliere* to Clinton. But after Election Day, they vacation in Venice and would later accept an advance of nearly $1 million for a she-did, he-did book on the race and exchange I-dos — proving that politics don't always make estranged bedfellows.

MADONNA confirmed that she was in a league of her own by way of a book that in bygone days would have been seen only at smokers, not in shopping mall windows. *Sex* put on display all of her 34-year-old anatomy solo, in tandem, in trios and in yet larger groups. Fittingly, perhaps, even the cover tended to fall off (not always to the pleasure of those who had forked over $49.95).

RICHARD YOUNG / REX

His master's voice did not let MACAULEY CULKIN down. Yes, Hollywood's MVP (Most Valuable Peewee), 12, was miscast in a close-but-no-cigar drama, *My Girl,* that was as rigor mortised as his character. But dad Kit, 49, also agreed to let his son appear in *Home Alone 2* for a screamer of a raise: from $100,000 for No. 1 to $4.5 million plus 5 percent of the gross of the sequel.

TIMOTHY GREENFIELD SANDERS / ONYX

Hissy fits notwithstanding, **MICHELLE PFEIFFER,** 35, rubbed audiences the right way in *Batman Returns.* Offscreen, she ended a relationship with character actor Fisher Stevens, 29, and in 1993, after adopting an infant daughter, married TV producer David (*L.A. Law, Picket Fences)* Kelley, 36.

WARNER BROS

Every breath they took, every rein he shook brought **STING,** 40, and **TRUDIE STYLER,** 38, closer to formalizing their synchronicity after 10 years and three kids. Plus, their $250,000 worth of Gianni Versace finery was slated to be auctioned off, with proceeds donated to Rainforest, the ecocharity that had become the ex-Police chief's favorite new nonmusical beat.

BRIAN ARIS / OUTLINE

The Abdominal Showman of rock gave up the security of being Mark Wahlberg, New Kid on the Block, to make his **MARKY MARK** as a rap soloist. At 20, the singer had an attitude that got him into trouble with Asians, gays and the other minorities he'd put down. More commercial was a crotch-grabbing, shorts-flaunting act that got him into ads for Calvin Klein.

LYNN GOLDSMITH / LGI

SHARON STONE sure made her point in *Basic Instinct.* The hit thriller jacked her fee from $500,000 to $4 mil per and also taught her to cut to the heart of personal matters (Stone, 34, dusted off one beau because he was less appealing than "a dirt sandwich"). Gee, maybe that's why so many spoke so well of her.

FIROOZ ZAHEDI / ONYX

What the long-range videotape of March 3, 1991, could not show: the damage wrought by the LAPD on **RODNEY KING.** Yet 13 months later in the suburb of Simi Valley, a jury with no black member acquitted four white cops. It took South Central Los Angeles only hours to blow. On Day 2 of the rioting, King, now 26, emerged from seclusion to plead, "Can we just all get along?" Not before 53 were dead, 2,383 injured and 17,000 arrested.

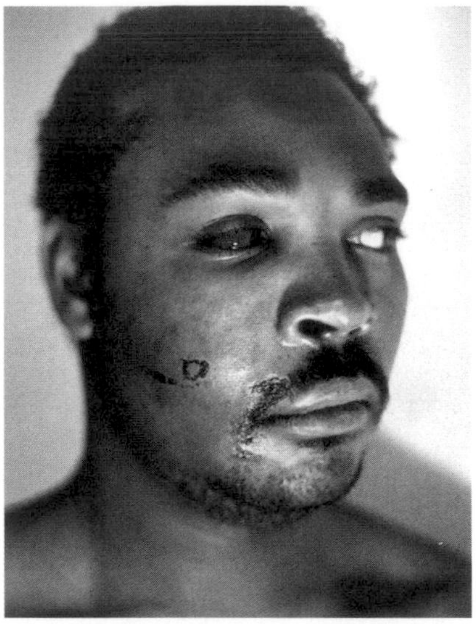

For an attractive woman in showbiz who was the constant target of flat-chest jokes (T-shirts with fried eggs, etc.), the fix seemed obvious: silicone. But by the time **JENNY JONES** turned 45 and had her own talk show, six sets of implants in 11 years (each to correct a prior failure) had left her breasts numb, hard and laced with unremovable silicone. Jones bravely went public and started a nonprofit support group for other women in a similar bad fix.

DANA FINEMAN / SYGMA

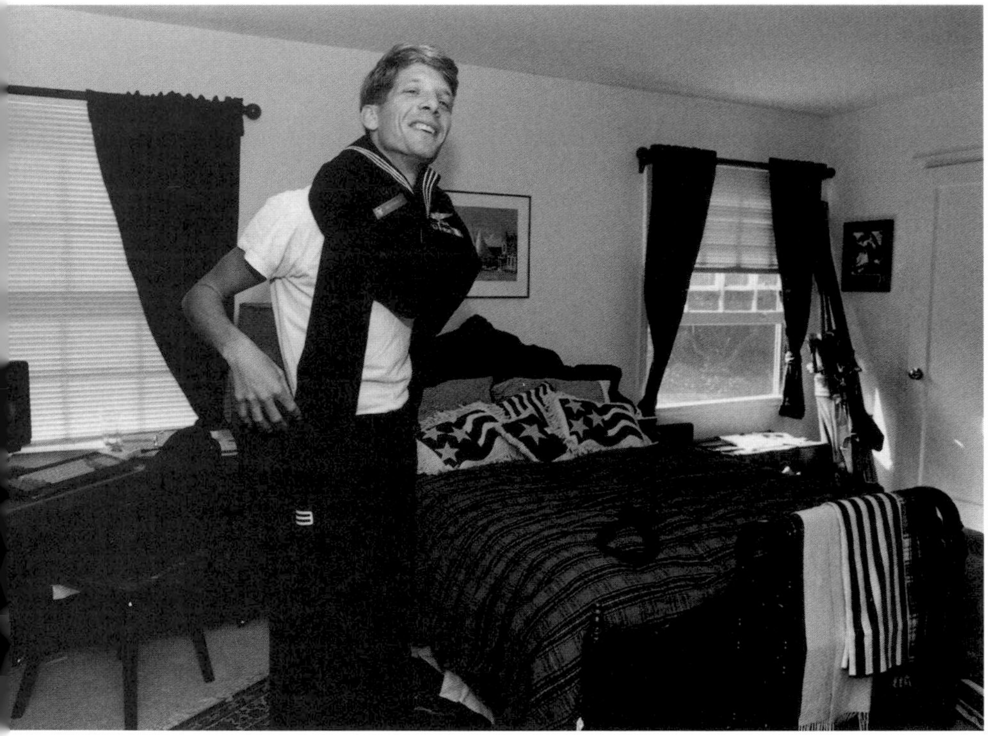

"I am, in fact, gay," said **KEITH MEINHOLD,** 30, on a national newscast. Soon, the naval sonar man was discharged despite top reviews during his 12-year-career. A federal judge ruled as unconstitutional the Navy's ban on gays and ordered him reinstated. In 1993, promoted to patrol-plane duty, he re-upped a third time—even as the Navy again sought the right to discharge him.

PENNI GLADSTONE

Her balance started to go while filming *Back to the Beach,* her 1987 retro reunion with Frankie Avalon, then her vision. Doctors told **ANNETTE FUNICELLO** she had a disease afflicting 350,000 Americans, two-thirds of them women—multiple sclerosis. For five years, the First Mouseketeer hid her condition. Then, at 49, Funicello revealed her MS in the hopes that her travails might help others.

HARRY BENSON

Eleven years into "The Marriage of the Century," the Waleses, on a four-day tour of South Korea, spoke a body language that needed no translation. At year's end, the Queen—whose *annus horriblis* included a divorce for Anne, a separation for Andrew and a disastrous fire at Windsor Castle—acceded also to the formal separation of **CHARLES** and **DIANA.**

THE SUN / REX USA

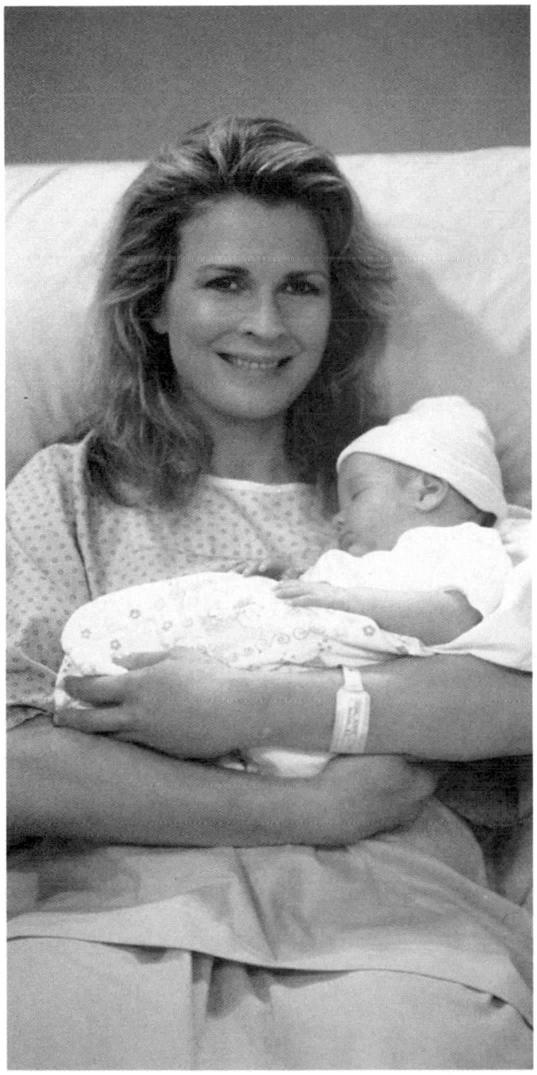

Only make-believe was the baby that *Murphy Brown's* writers had their bachelor girl bear. But the notion of glorifying unwed mothers was too much for Vice President Dan Quayle to bear; he even linked the L.A. riots to the birth of Avery Brown. Bad target selection: **CANDICE BERGEN,** 46, had Nielsen family values of 35 million viewers a week—and better writers to boot.

RICHARD CARTWRIGHT / CBS

Putting a bullet in the head of her lover's wife was no joke. Yet perhaps because the victim survived, the Long Island triangle—underage boy toy **AMY FISHER,** 17 (with lawyer **ERIC NAIBURG),** her lizard-booted Lothario, Joey Buttafuoco, 38, and his see-no-evil spouse, Mary Jo, 37—became a stand-alone punch line (and the subject of three made-for-TV quickies that were virtually simulcast). For shooting Mary Jo, Amy drew a 5-to-15-year term; for having statutorily raped Amy, Joey drew six months and a $5,000 fine.

DICK YARWOOD / NEWSDAY

With some 65 percent of the electorate wired for cable by the time of Campaign '92, small wonder that candidates increasingly sought the guest seat at the CNN studio where **LARRY KING,** 59, conducted his nightly hour-long cable schmooze. If they wanted a forum for thoughts that ran longer than a sound bite, this was one. And if they didn't, there were all those viewers' calls to make the time fly.

KIMBERLY BUTLER

By Election Day, anyone who still thought Texans were laconic had a busted TV. Between guest shots and infomercials that spread his I'm-mad-as-hell gospel, data-processing mogul and presidential hopeful **ROSS PEROT,** 62, hopped more dials than the Energizer Bunny. The $2.5-billionaire did a mysterious vanishing act for three months but re-entered the race and enjoyed the last laugh—by capturing 19 percent of the popular vote.

RICHARD DREW / ASSOCIATED PRESS

Today vets **JANE PAULEY** (*left,* 1976-1989), **KATIE COURIC** (1991-) and **BARBARA WALTERS** (1961-1976) stayed up until prime time to help the show observe its 40th birthday. Until Walters became coanchor in 1974, fellow alumnae like Estelle Parsons, Betsy Palmer and a pre-*Brady Bunch* Florence Henderson tended to handle the weather duties managed so ably since 1980 by Willard Scott.

HARRY BENSON

FOX
REALISTIC
STEREO CASSETTE RECORDER
STEREO-MATE
WCBS NEWSRADIO 88
WCBS NEWSRADIO 88

According to Mel Brooks's 2,000-Year-Old-Man, the hottest ticket at the World's Fair of his day allowed its purchaser to climb a cliff and then step off: "We called it *falling.*" Same ride, only with a different name, **BUNGEE JUMPING,** and a happier ending: Modern thrill-seekers bounced back.

JOHN STOREY

At the Barcelona Games, **EARVIN JOHNSON**'s very special alchemy was on full display—a far cry from the day 10 months earlier when he quit pro hoops after testing HIV positive (the result, he said, of not saying no to groupies). Buoyed by his play in the Dream Team's golden romp, he began to prep a comeback. But when other NBAers noted that hardwood combat can draw blood, Magic, 32, quietly re-retired for good.

LENNY IGNELZI / ASSOCIATED PRESS

Three decades after welcoming his first guest, Groucho Marx, **JOHNNY CARSON,** 66, became the missing linkster of midnight television. His last *Tonight Show* guest was himself, for a moist-eyed look at moments from the preceding 4,350 shows. After the King, the deluge: Even jokers with zilch air time were given late night shows.

JOSEPH DEL VALLE / NBC

1993

The King of Pop could still draw a crowd: **MICHAEL JACKSON**'s prime-time chat with Oprah about his ever-more-ghoulish looks (the skin disease vitiglio, he said) was a Nielsen blockbuster. But the self-styled Peter Pan grew old beyond his 35 years when one of his Lost Boys told of being molested by him. The singer's global tour fell apart and longtime sponsor Pepsi told him to beat it. After drug rehab in Europe, Jackson flew home to his California ranch, named Neverland, to await at least one court date in the new year.

HARRY BENSON

Turning in his $40,000-a-year Manhattan Assistant District Attorney badge after four years, **JOHN F. KENNEDY JR.** biked his gear out of a downtown bachelor pad and into the uptown apartment of **DARYL HANNAH**. The two 32-year-olds then slowly splashed their way across the islands of the South Pacific before flying home to wedding bells (his cousin Ted Jr.'s).

MARCEL THOMAS / SIPA PRESS

On weekend leave from her first movie in two years, **JULIA ROBERTS,** 25, traveled to Muncie, Indiana, to barefoot it down the aisle with ironic country crooner **LYLE** ("I Married Her Just Because She Looks Like You.") **LOVETT,** 35. Returning to the set of *The Pelican Brief,* she was toasted by a cast and crew decked out in gag T-shirts that read: "He's A Lovely Boy . . . But You Really Must Do Something About His Hair."

SYGMA

Nixon in '96. Tan, Rested & Ready!" is the logo on a popular gift T-shirt at the library honoring the 37th President in Yorba Linda, California. Ironically, 42nd President Bill Clinton runs into a couple of -gates of his own. Nannygate claims his first two choices for Attorney General, Zöe Baird, 40, and Kimba Wood, 49 (though, apparently, good ole boys will be boys; failure to promptly pay taxes for domestic help does not disqualify Bobby Ray Inman, 62, from nomination as Secretary of Defense). And at year's end, a scenario with elements of a John Grisham thriller — the suicide of a White House aide, vanished legal files detailing the Clintons' partnership in a failed Ozark resort, a White House stonewall — threatens to boil over into Whitewatergate.

Mississippiwatergate sadly sums up Middle America after 100 days of rain and floods leave 50 dead, 70,000 homeless and $12 billion in property damage. Insurers must soon pay out another $1 billion when Los Angeles burns again; this time it is the pricier 'hoods, victims of Santa Ana-whipped brushfires.

Women of the year: Hillary Rodham Clinton, 45, the new Ms. Goodwrench of the health-care industry; Ruth Bader Ginsburg, 60, the new High Court jurist (she and Sandra Day O'Connor receive matching shirts that read, "The Supremes"); Toni Morrison, 62, the new Nobel Laureate in Literature; and Lorena Bobbitt, 24, the new "Auntie Maim" (the Virginia manicurist wields a kitchen knife to turn her sleeping husband John, 27, into the Penis de Milo).

Israel extends an olive branch to its Palestinian population (by way of direct talks, 45 years after the Jewish state's founding) and accepts one from the Vatican (by way of diplomatic recognition, 1,960 years after the death of Christ).

Twelve years after being shot by John Hinckley Jr., Reagan press secretary James Brady, 53, returns to the White House to see Bill Clinton sign a law making it slightly harder to buy a pistol. Fernando Mateo, owner of a New York City carpet installation firm, offers $100 gift certificates from Toys "R" Us in exchange for guns; 1,500 accept (leaving only some 200 million firearms in circulation).

Passages: Contralto Marian Anderson, 96. Protean author Anthony (*A Clockwork Orange*) Burgess, 76. Raymond Burr, 76. Pierre Culliford, 64 (creator of the Smurfs). Cocaine kingpin Pablo Escobar Gaviria, 44 (shot dead by Colombian police). Moviemaker Federico Fellini, 73. Jazzman Dizzy Gillespie, 75. Silent-screen heroine Lillian Gish, 99. Helen Hayes, 92. Myrna Loy, 88. TV personality Garry Moore, 78. Rudolf Nureyev, 54 (of AIDS). Historian C. Northcote Parkinson, 83 (author of Parkinson's Law: Work expands to fill the available time). Physician-essayist Lewis (*The Lives of a Cell*) Thomas, 80. Country crooner Conway ("It's Only Make Believe") Twitty, 59. IBM patriarch Thomas Watson Jr., 79.

Can Steven Spielberg, 46, possibly top the monstrous velociraptors that screech his *Jurassic Park* to the top of the all-time box-office list? Yes, with the Nazis who run the forced-labor camp in *Schindler's List*. Finally, on Skywalker Ranch in Northern California, George Lucas, 49, is honing a three-part prequel to his *Star Wars* trilogy; it will have an all-new cast (is there a role for Mikhail Gorbachev, 62, who makes his movie debut in Wim Wenders's *Faraway, So Close*?) and, if successful, lead to Nos. 7, 8 and 9. That'd be a true Force majeure.

After 23 years at the University of Northern Iowa, business professor **ROBERT JAMES WALLER** took an unpaid leave and wrote his first novel, *The Bridges of Madison County* (middle-aged adultery in Iowa), in just two weeks. It was atop the best-seller list when he wrote No. 2, *Slow Waltz in Cedar Bend* (middle-aged adultery in Iowa and India) in just 10 days. Both were atop the list when the 54-year-old Waller, having gotten the hang of it, began Nos. 3, 4 and 5 simultaneously.

REX RYSTEDT

Vietnam noncombatant Bill Clinton took at least a verbal fragging in trying to end the Pentagon ban on gays. He fared better at persuading the Tailhook-embarrassed military to accept women combat pilots. No. 1 on the flight line: **JEANNIE FLYNN,** 26, who gladly traded in a T-38 trainer (*right*) for a shot at showing that she had the right stuff to top-gun an F-15E Strike Eagle.

CO RENTMEESTER

Feds raiding the Waco, Texas, ranch of a cult led by Messianic gun freak **DAVID KORESH** (né Vernon Howell), 33, set off a firefight that killed four agents and 15 Branch Davidians. After a 51-day siege, frustrated feds sent in armored vehicles, which ignited a fire that killed Koresh and 84 Davidians, a third of them children. Attorney General Janet Reno took responsibility, but the first reviews did not directly blame her.

WACO TRIBUNE HERALD / SYGMA

Having taken in the view from the top of the **WORLD TRADE CENTER,** 17 Brooklyn kindergartners and 55 adults were riding down when their elevator stopped and the lights went out. Only when rescued five hours later (*left*) did they learn the tower had been gutted by a bomb that killed six and injured 1,042. Authorities later arrested blind Sheik Omar Abdel Rahman, 55, who had somehow ducked a ban on entering the U.S., and six of his followers.

TIM RUNELS / CAMERA 5

RIVER PHOENIX keeled over outside an L.A. night club and was DOA at the hospital. The actor, 23, had sterling credits (*Stand by Me, Running on Empty, My Own Private Idaho)* and politically fashionable beliefs (he was a leather-shunning vegetarian who supported environmental causes). What killed him was a socially fashionable habit (an overdose of coke mixed with heroin).

MARK CONTRATTO / OUTLINE

Shortly after completing a UNICEF mercy mission to Somalia *(above),* **AUDREY HEPBURN** learned the extent of her illness. She had survived the divorce of her parents, the Nazi occupation of her native Holland and the marriage-ending stresses of megastardom; in just four months, though, one of Hollywood's fairest and most generous ladies was dead of cancer, at 63.

ROBERT WOLDERS/ SYGMA

Icarus flew too close to the sun. **MICHAEL JORDAN,** 30, clipped his own wings because he was a son too close to his father. Controversy over Jordan's high-stakes bets didn't stop him from leading the Chicago Bulls to an NBA title three-peat. But the brutal highway rest-stop murder of his dad and best pal, James, soon led the grieving Michael to ground future flights of Air Jordan.

MANNY MILLAN / SPORTS ILLUSTRATED

Tennis at the level reached by **ARTHUR ASHE**—'68 U.S. Open champ, '75 Wimbledon titleist—called for head and heart as well as pure skill. His rise from the segregated courts of Virginia taught him a tough-mindedness that extended to the disease he contracted from blood received during surgery in 1983. AIDS was not his greatest burden, said Ashe, who died of it at age 49: "Being black is."

MICHAEL O'NEILL / OUTLINE

In one of his movies, the phrase "self-absorbed, untrustworthy and insensitive" would surely trigger a punch line. But **WOODY ALLEN,** 55, could not laugh off that real-life characterization by a New York City judge who, citing the director's affair with Mia Farrow's daughter Soon-Yi Previn, 22, awarded Farrow, 48, custody of her son by Allen and curtailed his access to two children he had coadopted with her. Farrow then sued to take away even those rights.

MICHAEL ALBANS / ASSOCIATED PRESS

Had **JERRY SEINFELD**, 39, grown too small for his britches? Or was he just showing that he didn't need his NBC sitcom mates (or American Express straight men) to get a yuk? The comedian published *Seinlanguage,* a 180-page deliver-it-yourself stand-up kit, and—*Whoa!*—it became a best-seller even without Kramer skidding around the corner like a one-man rim shot.

BONNIE SCHIFFMAN / ONYX

And now, after 11 years, 275 episodes and 26 Emmys, it was time for *Cheers: Last Call.* Exiting left: **RHEA PERLMAN, TED DANSON, KIRSTIE ALLEY, JOHN RATZENBERGER, WOODIE HARRELSON, GEORGE WENDT** and **KELSEY GRAMMER** (who alone strutted right into another hit, the spin-off sitcom *Frasier).*

BRIAN LANKER / LIFE

BURT REYNOLDS, 57, and **LONI ANDERSON,** 46, enlivened the summer hiatus with a made-for-Court-TV family feud. Loni flirted with other men, claimed his pals. Her pals, in turn, pointed out that Burt had been carrying on for two years with a cocktail-lounge manager. So nasty was the break-up of the five-year marriage (complicated by adopted son **QUINTON,** 4) that it even cost Reynolds two lucrative endorsements.

HARRY BENSON

TED DANSON, 45, tried out some black comedy at a Manhattan roast for his *Made in America* costar, **WHOOPI GOLDBERG,** 43. Curiously, outrage was expressed by more white guests than black. More curiously, Goldberg said she wrote some of his slurry zingers. Still more curiously, the couple then publicly ended an affair they'd never confirmed—but added they would soon reteam to film *Remade in America.*

DIANE COHEN

In a nation that was 51.2 percent female, **HILLARY RODHAM CLINTON** talked up health care with the 6 percent of the Senate that was female: **CAROL MOSELEY-BRAUN** *(left),* **PATTY MURRAY, BARBARA MIKULSKI, BARBARA BOXER, DIANNE FEINSTEIN** and **NANCY KASSEBAUM.**

ROBERT TRIPPETT / SIPA PRESS

She left center stage as she had entered, pinned by kliegs and strobes and zeroed in the cross hairs of cameras. In 12 short years, **PRINCESS DIANA** had been hothouse-forced to become savvy in the demands of the public. Now she wanted to attend to other needs. At 32, a year after her separation from Charles (and pressured by his supporters), she announced her withdrawal from most royal duties to devote more private time to sons Wills, 11, and Harry, 9.

DAVID CHANCELLOR / ALPHA / GLOBE

Please **HAMMER** don't hurt 'em: **TIPPER GORE,** 44, was no longer the clean-lyrics crusader of the mid-'80s but the Second Lady, and didn't her hubby, 45, want everyone to call him **AL?** The Inaugural bash was as good a place as any to bury all outstanding hatchets.

IRA SCHWARTZ / REUTERS / UPI BETTMANN

HOWARD STERN, 39, author of the gross-out best-seller, *Private Parts,* lost his college deejay job over an offensive *Godzilla Goes to Harlem* skit (but he won wife **ALISON,** now 39 and mom to three preteen girls). Not until 1985 did Stern find a home for his King Leer act, which in syndication now earned him 3 million listeners daily, $2 million annually—and $1 million in career FCC fines.

JEFFREY LOWE

INDEX TO PICTURES

BILLIE JEAN KING, 1974 SUNNY BAK / SHOOTING STAR

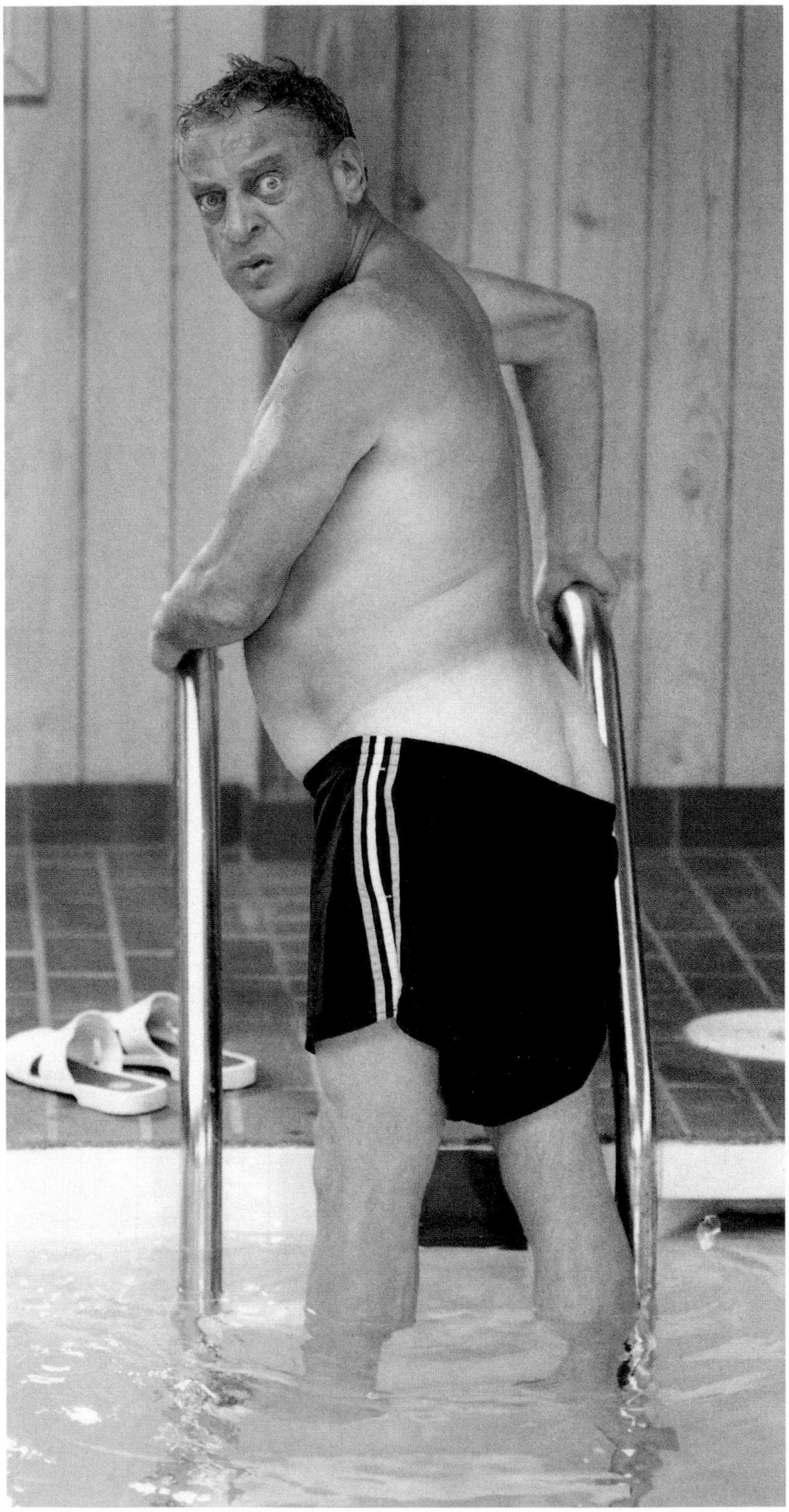

RODNEY DANGERFIELD, 1986

RAEANNE RUBENSTEIN